A. P. Driscoll Feb'84

TALK

1283

£8.95

D1002857

TALK

An Analysis of Speech and Non-Verbal Behaviour in Conversation

GEOFFREY BEATTIE

Open University Press

Milton Keynes

Open University Press
A division of
Open University Education Enterprises Limited
12 Cofferidge Close
Stony Stratford
Milton Keynes
MK11 1BY
England

First published 1983
Copyright © Geoffrey Beattie

All rights reserved. No part of this work may be reproduced in any form, by mimeograph or by any other means, without permission in writing from the publisher.

British Library Cataloguing in Publication Data

Beattie, Geoffrey
  Talk: an analysis of speech and non-verbal
  behaviour in conversation
  1. Psycholinguistics   2. Speech
  I. Title
  401'.0   BF455

ISBN 0-335-10414-2

Text design by W.A.P.

Filmset by Cambrian Typesetters
Aldershot, Hants.
Printed in Great Britain by M. & A.
Thomson Litho Limited,
East Kilbride, Scotland

DEDICATION

For my brother Bill who died on Nanda Devi,
September 1978

Contents

Contents

Interruptions in political interviews
Conclusions

7 Conclusions

Figures

Tables

Acknowledgements

I owe a debt of gratitude to many people. My colleagues, Brian Butterworth, Anne Cutler and Phil Barnard, all made major contributions to the research reported in this book. Professors Kevin Connolly and John Frisby at Sheffield offered a good deal of support, both in terms of providing excellent research facilities and by encouraging me to write. John Skelton, from the Open University Press, was enthusiastic about this book from the beginning and somehow managed to maintain his enthusiasm against the odds. Gay Rich typed the manuscript, and Lesley Speakman was invaluable in checking it repeatedly. Carol provided help and assistance, and critical advice, throughout the duration of the research and the writing.

Research never takes place in a vacuum. I was inspired by the work of the late Frieda Goldman-Eisler and Erving Goffman and they were kind enough to offer me a good deal of encouragement in my own research. I would like to offer them a belated thanks.

I would like to thank Mouton Publishers for permission to reproduce Tables I.I (*Linguistics* (1981) 19, 1165–83), 3.2, 3.3, 3.4, 3.5, and Figure 3.1 (from *Linguistics* (1979) **17**, 61–78), Tables 4.1–4.4 (from *Semiotica* (1978) **23**, 29–52), Tables 5.1–5.6 (from *Linguistics* (1979) **17**, 213–30), Table 5.7 (from *Semiotica* (1981) **34**, 55–70), Figure 6.1 and Tables 6.1–6.7 (from *Linguistics* (1981) **19**, 15–35), Tables 6.8–6.10 (from *Semiotica*, (1982) **39**, 93–114).

I would like to thank the British Psychological Society for permission to reproduce Tables 2.1 and 2.2 (from the *British Journal of Social Psychology*, **21**, 31–4), Table 3.1 (from the *British Journal of Social Psychology*, **20**, 243–8). I would like to thank the Plenum Publishing Corporation for permission to reproduce Tables 4.5–4.8 (from Campbell and Smith (1978)

Recent Advances in the Psychology of Language: Formal and Experimental Approaches). I would also like to thank Macmillan Journals Plc for permission to reproduce Tables 6.11 and 6.12, and Figures 6.10 and 6.11 (from *Nature*, 1982, **300**, 744–7).

Lastly, I would like to thank Anne Cutler for making Figures 6.10 and 6.11.

1

General introduction: language and nonverbal communication in natural conversation

Conversation, n. A fair for the display of the minor mental commodities, each exhibitor being too intent upon the arrangement of his own wares to observe those of his neighbor.

AMBROSE BIERCE
The Devil's Dictionary (1881–1911)

Conversation: foundation stone of the social world

If possession of a language is the most essentially human of all attributes, then the use of language in its appropriate social context must be the most essentially human of all activities. Human babies come into the world to be greeted by their mothers who often seem to start the relationship with talk ('Isn't she lovely?', 'What a big baby', etc.). The baby may just cry but the mother holds, looks, smiles and talks. Language comes flooding out of the mother in a cocoon of nonverbal behaviour. And this continues: over the first few years of life we learn to talk in the context of this conversational flow — adult speech is modified and continually directed towards the child (see Snow and Ferguson 1977). We act first — cry, grimace, look; learn to talk later. There is even evidence to suggest that the type of conversation held between the mother and child at age three months significantly affects later linguistic development – at least measured in terms of mean length of utterance at a certain age (Freedle and Lewis 1977). At the same time as this is going on we are constantly learning about the world – both physical and social – through this same conversational medium. For the rest of one's life, conversation plays an equally essential role. In order to find a mate, man may begin by using a few nonverbal signals at a distance but after a short time, nonverbal signals alone, even at close range, would not be sufficient, in the majority of cases. The silent language of love is not that silent – meaningful looks have to be accompanied by meaningful speech. When we are ill, face-to-face conversation is the medium through which we convey information about what is wrong; computer diagnosis is a very poor second. When we are depressed, common wisdom tells us that it would help if we talked to someone about it. Psychotherapy is founded on this principle. On the other hand, it has been suggested that we may become ill because of conversation. Gregory Bateson (1973) suggested that mental illness may develop if we are the recipient of a series of communications of an essentially contradictory nature. Schizophrenia, it was suggested, is a mode of 'coping' with the conflicting demands of a double-bind communication – a type of communication in which the two principal channels, verbal and nonverbal, are often in contradiction.

 Conversation is without doubt the foundation stone of the social world – human beings learn to talk *in* it, find a mate *with* it, are socialized *through* it, rise in the social hierarchy as a result *of* it, and, it is suggested, may even develop mental illness *because* of it. This book explores a small range of some of the issues of how speech and nonverbal behaviour relate and are used in natural conversation. Conversation is primarily a social event, perhaps the major social event between people, but complex cognitive processes are neverthe-less brought to bear on the planning and generation of the spontaneous speech within it. These complex psycholinguistic pro-cesses will be considered in detail in this book. The book will have therefore both a social and a cognitive flavour.

The very centrality of conversation guarantees its place in the interests of interlocking disciplines – psychology, linguistics and sociology. Psychologists have been interested in the study of conversation not just because of its importance for cognitive and social development, but also for its potential importance for clinical psychology. Many clinically identifiable groups find social interaction, and indeed some of the most basic processes of conversation, highly problematic (see Trower, Bryant and Argyle 1978). Such difficulty can result in social isolation and may in time cause severe mental illness. Processes of conversation have been described by psychologists as social skills, analogous to motor skills such as driving a car (see Argyle and Kendon 1967), skills at which many groups appear deficient. Psychologists would like to be able to describe and identify those skills so that groups deficient in them could be trained to behave appropriately. The typical focus of psychologists on conversation has been the non-linguistic aspects of communication – the nonverbal behaviour which accompanies language (Argyle 1967), or the structural features of conversation like turn-taking (see Duncan and Fiske 1977). Linguists, on the other hand, certainly during the Chomskian era, seemed to neglect the study of natural conversation, instead focussing on idealized and abstract data bases – speaker-hearers' intuitions of well-formed syntactic units of language (Chomsky 1965). The explicit aim was to construct grammars of linguistic competence which may or may not have a direct bearing on actual linguistic performance (see, for example, Fodor, Bever and Garrett 1974, for one attempt to map out the connections). However, in recent years, there has been an increasing tendency to reconsider units of language larger than the sentence – to attempt to construct text grammars (see Van Dijk 1977) and to consider the devices used to connect sentences (see Halliday and Hasan 1976). Conversation yields such data in abundance, even if it sometimes can be hard to extract, and as a result, conversation has become a popular area of concern in contemporary linguistics. For that branch of sociology most directly concerned with natural conversation – ethnomethodology (see Garfinkel 1967) – conversation is simply there (see Schegloff and Sacks 1973), and like the mountain for the mountaineer, is therefore a challenge. They accord no theoretical primacy to conversation as a type of interaction. Despite this, however, ethnomethodology was perhaps the first discipline to highlight the real complexity of some of the most basic processes of conversation like the exchange of turns at talk, and to attempt to derive a mechanism of sufficient power to be able to describe and explain some of these processes (see Sacks, Schegloff and Jefferson 1974).

The real problem, however, with the study of conversation is that the different disciplines have concentrated on very different aspects of conversations, and no real synthesis has been attempted. Psychologists have made some headway at identifying the role of various specific nonverbal behaviours like eye-gaze, posture and gesture in conversation, but have not really attempted to connect the description of these behaviours to any detailed analysis of the linguistic aspects of the conversation. For example, in Adam Kendon's (1967) seminal paper

on the role of eye-gaze in turn-taking in conversation, the sole
linguistic unit employed in the analysis of turn-taking was 'utterance'
– a term not even defined in the paper. Linguists have made some
headway at identifying how syntactic units of language, like the
clause, may bind together to form larger units of more relevance to
conversation (see Halliday and Hasan 1976), but the social and
psychological reality of these units has been ignored. How are these
units planned? Are clauses independent units of planning and
production in conversation? Is spontaneous speech conceptualized in
primarily semantic or syntactic units? Ethnomethodologists have
successfully highlighted the complexity of some of the more basic
processes of social interaction and have attempted to derive general
rules for accounting for these processes. Following the pioneering
work of Harvey Sacks, Emmanuel Schegloff and Gail Jefferson
(1974), it is quite clear that even some of the apparently simple
processes of conversation are highly complex and extremely skilfully
executed. But so often in the ethnomethodological account the role of
specific nonverbal signals in the execution and management of
conversation is omitted or ignored. And even the precise role of
specific linguistic cues is left somewhat vague. For example, Sacks *et
al.* tell us that intonation is important in the regulation of turn-taking
in conversation (see p. 722), but exactly how important is it?
Kendon's research in psychology has suggested that nonverbal signals
like eye-gaze are also important in this process, but how do these fit
into the Sacks *et al.* framework? Do nonverbal signals operate
independently of specific linguistic context? Do they carry a universal
significance or are they only important at certain points in speech?

The aim of this book is to begin an exploration of some of these
issues, to tie together the analysis of language and nonverbal
behaviour – to see how they act together in conversation. A primary
tool is the microanalysis of video-recordings or audio-recordings of
natural conversation – university supervisions, tutorials and seminars,
telephone calls, and televised political interviews. These are all natural
in that they do not owe their existence to the presence of the
conversational analyst. The research reported in the book asks the
fundamental question of how spontaneous speech is geared to the
demands of conversation. It asks specific questions about the nature of
units of encoding of spontaneous speech and the basic necessity for
hesitations in speech for cognitive planning. It also explores how the
structure of a speaker's nonverbal behaviour relates to the encoding of
spontaneous speech (see also McNeill 1979, for a related attempt to do
the same sort of thing). An additional aim is to outline some of the
rules and signals which govern the structure of natural conversation.

It attempts to identify both the visually transmitted nonverbal cues and the cues carried in the speech wave-form itself, such as intonation, which are responsible for the regulation of conversational exchanges. The research has thus elements in common with all three disciplines previously mentioned – psychology, linguistics and sociology.

The book derives from a series of empirical investigations published between 1978 and 1982. These investigations tried to mould a very complex data base, that is, the behaviour of speakers in conversation, into some kind of form – bit by bit, section by section, stage by stage. The goal is to identify structures and organizational principles linking speech and nonverbal behaviour: structures and principles that when identified will ultimately simplify a very complex data base.

Language and nonverbal communication: functional differences?

A major theoretical issue raised by this research is the relationship between language and nonverbal communication (NVC). Both are clearly important aspects of conversation but they have often been kept quite separate, on apparently conceptual and functional grounds, in the psychological literature. A fundamental thesis of this book will be that the apparent functional separateness of these two main components of communication is more illusory than real, and that when we attempt to analyse and understand something as complex as conversation we do not gain anything by arbitrarily separating the components before abandoning one or the other (depending upon which academic discipline one happens to be working in). Clearly, one of the first considerations of the book is therefore to examine the evidence for the functional distinctiveness of language and NVC.

It has been said that 'Humans use two quite separate languages, each with its own function' (Argyle and Trower 1979, p. 22). This is a rather extreme version of the more familiar claim that 'In human social behaviour it looks as if the NV (nonverbal) channel is used for negotiating interpersonal attitudes while the verbal channel is used primarily for conveying information' (Argyle 1967, p. 49). This suggests that the nonverbal channel – the silent channel of eye contact, head nods, gestures, posture, interpersonal distance, winks, fidgetings and eyebrow raisings carries out essentially social functions while the verbal channel of words and sentences primarily conveys semantic information. This is a classic distinction which proved in many ways to be a useful heuristic for guiding research in the field. There have been considerable advances in the understanding of the role of nonverbal behaviour in the development and maintenance of human social relationships (see Argyle 1974, for example). But even good heuristics can sometimes lead one astray. Perhaps psychologists, interested in the social aspects of conversation, devoted too much of their time and energy to the silent channel and not enough to verbal behaviour, the very essence of human social behaviour.

Perhaps the time has come to pause and examine the accuracy of this important claim. Intuitively it seems fine. The verbal channel, that is to say, speech, is after all very good at conveying semantic information; the nonverbal channel is much less useful in this respect. Of course, there are special nonverbal languages specifically designed to convey semantic information such as the languages of the deaf. And in noisy environments, where speech becomes problematic, nonverbal signals can substitute efficiently and effectively for speech if only in a limited domain (head nods, shrugs, two fingers for two or victory, etc.). However, these accomplishments are dwarfed by the enormous range and flexibility of verbal language which is a system with incredibly complex rules governing possible utterances – a rule system involving a series of universal principles which are thought to be innate to all human beings (see Chomsky 1976, but see also Beattie 1979e). Therefore Argyle's view on the primacy of the verbal channel in conveying semantic information is probably beyond question. However, the view that NVC is of paramount importance in the negotiation of interpersonal attitudes is perhaps open to some doubt. Argyle's claim is one of those parts of psychology which makes some intuitive sense – it would seem intuitively reasonable that we communicate our attitudes to another person by means by nonverbal signals (eye contact, degree of smiling, interpersonal distance etc.). In addition, a psychologist has carried out a number of seemingly compelling experiments which decide the issue. In this particular case the experiments in question were carried out by Michael Argyle and his co-workers (Argyle, Salter, Nicholson, Williams and Burgess 1970; Argyle, Alkema and Gilmour, 1971). They purported to show a marked difference in the power of NVC and language in the communication of interpersonal attitudes.

The methodology of these experiments is both well-known and fairly straightforward. Very briefly, three verbal messages (hostile, neutral or friendly in one experiment; superior, neutral or inferior in another) are delivered in each of three different nonverbal styles, care being taken at the outset to ensure that the verbal message and the nonverbal style of each kind have approximately the same effects on listener evaluation on certain specific dimensions. The combined communications are then rated on the same scales. The results apparently demonstrate quite clearly that the nonverbal channel greatly outweighs the verbal channel in the combined communication. Friendly verbal messages delivered in a hostile manner are perceived as very hostile, etc.

Let us, however, consider some possible limitations of these studies:

1. Firstly, in order to attempt to measure the relative importance of language and NVC, the strength of the two channels had to be controlled at the outset. They had to be equal in strength when measured independently. These studies therefore tell us about people's perceptions of a certain class of communications with the range of the strength of the components artifically set. The studies of course do not tell us anything about the range of effects produced by language and NVC in the world at large. Perhaps in the real world people do not use such obvious friendly or unfriendly or superior or inferior verbal messages, e.g. the inferior verbal message in the Argyle *et al.* (1970) study was 'These experiments must seem rather silly to you and I'm afraid they are not really concerned with anything very interesting and important. We'd be very glad if you could spare us a few moments afterwards to tell us how we could improve the experiment. We feel that we are not making a very good job of it, and feel rather guilty about wasting the time of busy people like yourself.' Is such a verbal statement ever likely to be said, except as a joke? Alternatively, perhaps the study was forced to employ exaggerated styles of NVC in order to balance with the language styles totally outside the range we find in the real world. The hostile nonverbal message was 'harsh voice, frown with teeth showing, tense posture'. Is this common? realistic? plausible? A demonstration that the types of language and NVC used in these studies approximate and indeed are representative of those found outside the laboratory world, would make the studies much more compelling.

2. One striking feature of both studies is that only one encoder was used – 'an ATTRACTIVE, FEMALE student aged 23'. In other words, encoders are treated as fixed effects (see Clark 1973). We do not know if the results can be generalized to encoders generally. What about male encoders? Does sex of encoder affect the outcome? We now know that there are important sex differences in the ability to use NVC and we certainly know that women are better at decoding NVC than men (see Hall 1978). Whether they are also better at encoding feelings and attitudes via NVC is more equivocal (see Hall 1979).

I recently attempted to replicate the Argyle *et al.* (1971) study following the original procedure very closely but using both a female

and male encoder (only one of each). Ten students rated separately the
original Argyle *et al.* friendly, neutral and hostile messages, which
were typed out, and the three nonverbal styles (the two encoders
reading numbers in a friendly, neutral or hostile manner) on six 7-
point scales. This was to ensure approximately equal strengths. In the
actual experiment 16 female and 14 male students rated the 18
combined communications (9 from each encoder) presented on
videotape. The results were striking. Here I will only consider the
results on the hostile–friendly dimension. For the female encoders the
results came out as expressed – the nonverbal style outweighed verbal
content, but for the male encoder this 'typical' pattern did not emerge.
(See Table 1.1 which includes Argyle *et al.*'s (1971) results for
comparison.)

In the case of the female encoder the hostile verbal message
delivered in a friendly nonverbal style was perceived as significantly
more friendly than a friendly verbal message in a hostile nonverbal
style for both male (Wilcoxon matched pairs signed-ranks test,
$T = 10 \cdot 5$, $n = 13$, $p < 0 \cdot 05$, 2-tailed test) and female decoders
($T = 0$, $n = 15$, $p < 0 \cdot 005$, 2-tail). In the case of male encoders there
was no significant difference for either male ($T = 18$, $n = 11$, n.s., 2-
tail) or female decoders ($T = 11$, $n = 9$, n.s., 2-tail). In other words,
in the case of male encoders not only does the nonverbal component
not greatly outweigh verbal content, it does not even appear reliably
stronger across decoders.

Clearly, this study has all the faults of the original – encoders for
example are again treated as fixed effects. I introduced it to highlight
my concern about the use of only one female in the original study.
(Perhaps we also attend more to the nonverbal behaviour of attractive
people than to unattractive people, it would be interesting to see if the
effects also generalized to the old and ugly!)

3.   My third reservation concerns the fact that decoders in such
experiments are compelled to attend to the communication. In real life
people are not usually compelled to attend to behaviour to such an
extent. We can go to the extreme of putting our fingers in our ears to
shut out what people are saying or we can simply not listen. It is
perhaps even easier to shut out NVC than language by simply averting
eye-gaze. Ralph Exline (1971) demonstrated that people are more
likely to avert eye-gaze when someone has just said something
negative to them. How do people behave, in terms of attention, when
others are being friendly or hostile towards them? And how do
patterns of attention change with various combinations of language
and NVC? If most facial expressions are fairly fleeting (see Ekman and
Friesen 1969) are we likely to miss many of the nonverbal expressions

Table 1.1 Mean ratings of messages on hostile—friendly
dimensions for male and female encoders

Female encoder

Verbal		Nonverbal	
	Friendly	*Neutral*	*Hostile*
Friendly	6.1	5.2	2.1
Neutral	5.2	4.4	1.8
Hostile	5.2	3.3	1.7

Female encoder (Argyle et al. 1971)

Verbal		Nonverbal	
	Friendly	*Neutral*	*Hostile*
Friendly	6.03	4.27	1.60
Neutral	6.03	4.10	1.37
Hostile	5.17	2.83	1.80

Male encoder

Verbal		Nonverbal	
	Friendly	*Neutral*	*Hostile*
Friendly	4.9	5.1	3.9
Neutral	5.1	4.6	2.6
Hostile	4.7	2.9	2.4

of hostility but find it impossible to avoid the explicit verbal message of hostility being hammered into consciousness? In Argyle's experiments attentional shifts which may be important in decoding communication in the real world are not tapped. Furthermore, what about our memory of events? Presumably we can remember the details of explicit verbal communication better than nonverbal style (which will presumably just leave us with a vague 'feeling'). Perhaps after some time has elapsed we may reassess the communication. 'I thought she was being very unfriendly but she did say she liked me', etc. This kind of thing does seem to happen. NVC may have more immediate effect than language but if we assume that communication is important in the development of human relationships then memory for communication (and perhaps even the mental reliving of important episodes) may also be significant. Language, it may be supposed, is likely to have a profound effect on our memory of events and may with time become more significant.

4.   My fourth reservation concerns the vocal accompaniments of

language (stress, tone, patterns of hesitation, etc.). Argyle has viewed them as part of NVC. Most linguists would, however, like to make a distinction between some of these elements – paralanguage (pauses, hesitations, etc.) and prosody (intonation and stress) – on the basis of their relative integration with language (see Lyons 1972). Prosodic elements are most closely integrated with language and most linguists would wish to include prosody as an essential element of language. The point about the Argyle *et al.* experiments is that 'language' there means the words alone and this aspect is contrasted with everything else – visible NVC and all verbal aspects of language, some of which are surely prosodic in nature. The friendly nonverbal style for example had as one component 'a soft tone of voice' compared with an 'expressionless voice' in the neutral style. Prosodic elements would therefore have been varied but categorized as variations in NVC. If we accept that prosody should be regarded as an essential element of the linguistic channel then the Argyle studies do not provide accurate estimates of the relative strength of language and NVC in the communication of interpersonal attitudes at all.

The general point I am making is a simple one. These experiments by Argyle were ingenious and important but we must be extremely wary about generalizing the conclusions of these studies to all human social interaction. All experiments have limitations. In my view the limitations of these particular experiments are severe. Language is a very subtle medium, but its subtlety was not tapped in these experiments. Language conveys semantic information in subtle ways, but it also conveys interpersonal attitudes in equally subtle ways. Word choice, syntax, topic, theme, all undoubtedly carry hidden messages about interpersonal attitudes, in addition to simultaneously transmitting semantic information. 'Come in Miss Jones. Do take a seat. I want to discuss with you why you've been absent for the past three days' and 'Hi Lesley, where've you been?' may elicit the same semantic information in a particular social context but these messages undoubtedly transmit different information, in the interpersonal domain, both to the addressee and to anyone else who might be listening. Psychologists have perhaps been slow at studying how language operates so effectively in the interpersonal domain. This endeavour has been left to playwrights, novelists, poets, even linguists. Psychologists interested in interpersonal behaviour have perhaps concentrated too much on the silent channel and not enough on the noisy, rich, complex verbal channel which structures, guides and constrains most human social interaction. This book will not have a great deal to say about how interpersonal attitudes are communicated by the two channels (and so in that sense it will not attempt to redress the imbalance in the research) but it will hopefully have something to say about how speech and nonverbal behaviour interact generally. Such an understanding could be seen as a necessary precursor to the unravelling of the social matrix.

At the beginning of this section, I mentioned two quotations from Michael Argyle. I have concentrated on evaluating one of these – the less extreme of the two. The first quotation is more extreme and in my view more misleading to those interested in the study of human social behaviour. The quotation again is 'Humans use two quite separate languages, each with its own function' (Argyle and Trower 1979, p. 22). This quotation drives linguists and psychologists apart. It says that the two languages of humans are 'separate' (and therefore separable) and each has its own function. But is it correct? When people converse, speech is emitted along with a good deal of nonverbal behaviour. Speakers glance at the listener and glance away. They gesture, they change posture, they twitch. To what extent are the two systems separable? It is a common observation that when someone makes a telephone call, they still often gesture with their free hand and you still get changes in direction of eye-gaze, despite the recipient of the communication being, in some cases, thousands of miles away. We seem programmed to act when we talk. You *can* force someone to sit with their arms folded and speak but if you let them speak spontaneously and give them a free choice about their own actions, then you will see them move. Moving and speaking seem to be closely related. We do not yet know the neural mechanisms underlying and connecting the processes of speech and gesture but such ignorance should not distract us from observing the essential connectedness of these two great complex systems. This book will not treat the verbal and nonverbal systems as separate and separable but as connected and connectable.

The claim about the functional distinctiveness of language and nonverbal communication would anyhow seem to be incorrect. Argyle (1978) outlined the four main functions of NVC. The first is the communication of interpersonal attitudes. We have covered this already. NVC does it, language does it, this function is therefore not unique to one system.

The second function of NVC outlined by Argyle in 1978 is the communication of affect. There is quite a tradition in the psychological literature of the demonstration of the importance of the nonverbal channel in the communication of emotion and affect generally. Mehrabian estimated that only 7% of the communication of affect is accomplished via the verbal channel, whereas 38% is carried in the paralinguistic channel and 55% in the visible channel (Mehrabian 1972). However, the studies on which these estimates were made all used posed, context-free nonverbal channels. Mehrabian himself explicitly mentioned that the findings of these studies should only be generalized with great caution although others have taken these figures as precise estimates of the contribution made by the three channels in communication (e.g. Brooks and Emmert 1976; Leathers 1976; see also Krauss, Apple, Morency, Wenzel and Winton 1981). Mehrabian and Wiener indeed pointed out:

> These findings regarding the relative contribution of the tonal component of a verbal message can be safely extended only to communication situations in which no additional information about the communicator—addressee relationship is available.
>
> (Mehrabian and Wiener 1967, p. 113)

However, a number of additional qualifications need to be made. Firstly, it may be unwise to treat all emotions or all types of affect as a unidimensional concept. Burns and Beier (1973) for example, found that certain emotions (e.g. happiness or anger) were more accurately communicated through visible cues, whereas others (e.g. fear) were more accurately communicated through vocal cues. Secondly, in a recent study by Krauss *et al.* (1981) which involved analysis of the relative contribution of verbal, vocal and visible channels of communication to the judgement of emotion in a vice-presidential debate and in personal interviews, Krauss *et al.* found no support for the assumption that nonverbal channels (vocal or visible information) form the primary basis for the communication of affect. Clearly, the original specific estimates made by Mehrabian were somewhat premature and indeed it is clear that the whole question of the relative importance of verbal and nonverbal communication in the communication of emotion and affect is very much a live (and unresolved) issue. Recognition of the non-unidimensionality of emotion and of the possible role of situational factors (see Krauss *et al.*, 1981, p. 319) must surely be a step in the right direction.

Returning to the question of the possible functional differences between language and NVC, the relevant point here is that no one would dispute that language can be used to encode emotion and thus the communication of emotion also cannot be a unique function of NVC.

The third function outlined by Argyle in 1978 is 'supporting speech'. According to Argyle,

> NVC supports speech in three ways: a) completing and elaborating on verbal utterances, b) providing evidence of attentiveness on the part of

listeners, and giving immediate feedback, and c) managing the synchronizing of utterances. (Argyle, 1978, p. 552)

By definition, (a) cannot be a unique function of NVC, (b) could be, but is not since there are a whole range of verbal signals of attentiveness which listeners use, often termed 'back channels' (mmm, yeah; see Duncan 1972; Yngve 1970). One interesting feature of these back channels is their precise positioning in conversation – for example, they rarely overlap with the current speaker's verbalizations (Dittmann and Llewellyn 1968).

With respect to (c), perhaps we have a more likely candidate. After all, it makes sense conceptually for NVC alone to be responsible for the synchronizing of utterances. This is not a trivial aspect of interaction because turn-taking in conversation, where participants take turns at holding the floor alone for a limited period, is such a central feature of conversation. It seems to be one of the basic organizational principles and it has even been described as a linguistic universal (Miller 1963). Despite its universality there is a considerable body of evidence to suggest that certain clinical groups are poor at it. It has thus become an important component of social skills training. Poor turn-taking skills seem to characterize a number of social groups. For example, one of the major differences between shy people and others is the ability of the latter to initiate and structure conversations (see Pilkonis 1977). The shy individuals have longer pauses between turns, and speak less frequently and for shorter periods of time. Conversations involving schizophrenics have also been shown to show marked disruption in turn-taking (see Chapple and Lindemann 1942; Matarazzo and Saslow 1961; but see also Rutter 1977a and 1977b for evidence that the typical poor performance of schizophrenics in turn-taking may be confined to clinical interviews on personal matters). Trower *et al.* (1978) also found poor turn-taking skills in neurotic patients diagnosed as socially unskilled:

Their speech lacked continuity and was punctuated by too many silences; they failed to hand over or take up the conversation and generally did little or nothing to control the interaction, leaving the other person to make all the moves (p. 50).

Depressed people also show disruption of turn-taking, as Libet and Lewinsohn 1973 note:

the available evidence indicates that 'the depressed person's timing of social responses is off' (p. 311).

The earliest research in psychology on this aspect of conversational interaction suggested that nonverbal signals were indeed responsible for regulating the floor. In fact I have argued (see Beattie 1980a) that the earliest studies on how participants manage to regulate conversation were based on an implicit 'traffic signal' conceptual framework – the signals used to regulate conversation were thought to possess universal significance, were obligatory in their operation (like traffic lights) and nonverbal in nature. Kendon (1967) compared the listener's (q's) response to the speaker (p), when p ended his utterance with or without gaze ('utterance' was not defined in the original paper but was subsequently defined as 'complete in form and content', and, in addition, marked by a change in topic: Kendon 1978; see also Beattie 1978a). Listener responses were categorized as 'q fails to respond, or pauses before responding' and 'q responds without a pause'. Kendon observed that if the utterance terminated with speaker gaze, listeners were more likely to respond without a pause than if it did not. In subsequent interpretations of this study, speaker gaze seems to have been regarded like a traffic signal telling listeners when to respond – 'floor apportionment is also requested by eye movements which act as signals of a speaker's intention' (Argyle 1974, p. 202). Of course, gaze was not as efficient as a traffic signal in that there were a number of instances in the Kendon study when the signal did not come on and when the listener set off immediately (29.3% of all immediate listener responses followed utterances terminating without speaker gaze). Moreover, in some cases, when the light turned green the listener failed to move off. This 'traffic light' approach has found its way into the clinical literature. Thus, one treatment which Trower *et al.* (1978) suggest for poor turn-taking skills in conversation is 'ask the other a question and continue looking at him, this may include leaning forward'.

Kendon's early research did indeed suggest that turn-regulation is accomplished by nonverbal signals. But I will present evidence in this book (see Chapter 5) that this view was far too simple and that complex interaction effects between language and nonverbal signals are actually the crucial cues.

The fourth function of NVC outlined by Argyle (1978) is self-presentation. Argyle says:

> It is performed mainly by clothes and other aspects of appearance, and by voice and general style of behaviour (p. 552).

But in *Social Interaction* (1974) Argyle outlines some of the verbal means of self-presentation and particularly the indirect verbal means such as 'name-dropping'. Argyle (1975) indeed says that

> It is however quite common for people to engage in self-presentaion by indirect verbal methods (p. 384).

Four functions of NVC but none UNIQUE to NVC. Language can and does fulfil all four functions. Sometimes NVC fulfils the specific function to a greater extent, sometimes it does not. The claim that 'Humans use two quite separate languages, each with its own function' is, I think, demonstrably untrue.

The organization of speech and nonverbal behaviour in conversation

In my view we gain little from the argument which says that at the earliest opportunity we should separate the two main systems of communication and study them separately. In this book we will try the opposite strategy of investigating how they operate together. In limited contexts and in limited ways yes, but together nonetheless. Lest it be thought that the author is trying to claim the position of unique insight, it should be added immediately that the research to be reported in this book fits into a long tradition of research, by such workers as William Condon, Albert Scheflen and Adam Kendon. Those specific aspects of the author's own research which differentiate it from these others in the same field will become clearer later.

William Condon began exploring the interconnections between speech and nonverbal behaviour several decades ago. In 1967 he said:

> Language, in its natural occurrence as speech, is never disembodied but is always manifested through behavior. For example: what does the lowering of the voice, 'while' the eyes widen, 'while' the brows raise, 'while' an arm and fingers move, 'while' the head lowers, 'while' a leg and foot shift, 'while' the face flushes, have to do with what was said or left unsaid? How is this modified by the equally complex configurations of change which immediately precede and follow? And how are all of the above changes, in turn, related to the similarly involved behavior of the other person or persons in the interaction?
>
> We are quite often very clear about what a person said and meant but cannot tell precisely how he accomplished it or how we are able to accomplish our understanding of it.
>
> The search for the units of behaviour, their organisation and their empirical validation thus constitutes *the* central problem of behavioral analysis.
>
> (Condon and Ogston 1967, p. 221)

Condon and Ogston concentrated their search at the syllabic level using a sound movie film taken at 48 frames per second. They transcribed all of the phonemes of speech and the behaviour of extensive parts of the body such as the head, eyes, brows, upper lip, lower lip, trunk, right shoulder, right elbow, right wrist, first second and third finger on right hand and right thumb on to complex and detailed charts. Their search was detailed and exhaustive but was rewarded.

> During the intensive microanalysis of the three-person interaction . . . a startling discovery was made. The father and son were found to share patterns of bodily changes in a precise harmony with the mother as she spoke. These changes occurred in both in relationship to the mother at exactly the same frame (½₄ of a second). All three sustained directions of change across syllable and word length segments of speech and changed together at the same ½₄ of a second that these segments ended, to again sustain directions of movement together across the next ensuing segment. This occurred throughout the two utterances examined and in all other films of 'normal' interaction subsequently studied.
>
> (Condon and Ogston 1967, p. 229)

This phenomenon was dubbed interactional synchrony by Condon and Ogston and was, they argued, a basic organizational principle linking people in social interaction. An even more primitive principle was also observed, that of self-synchrony – 'The organisation of change of a speaker's body motion occurs synchronously with the articulated, segmental organisation of his speech. The body dances in time with speech' (Condon and Ogston 1967, p. 225).

In another investigation, involving a schizophrenic, Condon and Ogston found that interactional synchrony still occurred between the patient and his therapist but that self-synchrony partially broke down in that certain parts of the body were out of synchrony with certain other parts (Condon and Ogston 1966). The painstaking analyses of Condon and Ogston suggested that there are close organizational ties binding speech and nonverbal behaviour together at the most microscopic of levels. Organizational ties founded in the syllabic structure of speech are probably essential for successful communication.

The connections between language and nonverbal behaviour at more macro levels were explored by Albert Scheflen and Adam Kendon. Albert Scheflen was principally interested in the analysis of psychotherapy sessions. His goal was the description of the hierarchical structure of nonverbal behaviour and he took his lead from linguists and linguistic studies of the structure of language.

> Observed through time, the behaviors that make up communicative programs appear to be a continuous stream of events, but actually they are grouped into standard units of structure. These units are not arbitrary divisions made up spontaneously by an interactant or imposed

presumptively by an investigator; they are specific constellations of behavior built into a culture, learned and perceived in communication as Gestalten.

(Scheflen 1964, p. 319)

Scheflen attempted to describe the hierarchical structure of nonverbal behaviour corresponding to the hierarchical structure of language – the 'point' (a fixed head posture corresponding crudely to a point in discussion); a 'position' (a gross postural shift involving at least half the body and lasting from about half a minute to 5 or 6 minutes and corresponding to a point of view that an interactant may take in a given interaction); and a 'presentation' ('the totality of one person's positions in a given interaction'). Through his investigations of psychotherapy sessions he discovered a phenomenon related to interactional synchrony which he termed postural congruence – where two or more individuals adopt identical or mirror-image postures. Scheflen also noted how in group psychotherapy sessions members of the group not only took up similar postures but also shifted posture after one of them had changed position so that the group maintained postural congruence through a series of changes in body position. Scheflen also suggested that old friends who have long-term ties 'sometimes shift into postural congruence at times when they are temporarily arguing or taking opposing sides, as if to indicate the ultimate continuity of their relationship' (Scheflen 1964, p. 328). Again we have hints of strong interconnections between speech and nonverbal behaviour as well as *speculation* about the duality of functioning of the two systems. When friends argue verbally they compensate nonverbally by adopting identical postures, so Scheflen says. Once again, Scheflen's work attempts to come to grips with the complexity of conversation by dealing with the interaction between the main systems.

Very much in the Scheflen mould is some of the work of Adam Kendon who also described the relationship between speech and nonverbal behaviour at a fairly high level. Unfortunately, Kendon introduces a new terminology again. For dividing up language he used the terms: 'discourse' (the highest level unit), 'the locution cluster' (corresponding to a paragraph in written language), 'the locution group' (a group of locutions or complete sentences) and 'the locution' (a complete sentence separated by a 'distinct pause' from any immediately preceding locution). Kendon, like Scheflen, studied the relationship between the hierarchical structure of language and the hierarchical structure of behaviour. He found that

> The larger the speech unit, the greater the difference in the form of movement and the body parts involved. For example, the locution

groups were distinguished by the limb or limbs involved in gesticulation. Each locution was distinguished by a different pattern of movement within the same limb . . . Prior to each speech unit there is a change in position of one or more body parts. This was termed 'speech preparatory' movement. The larger the speech unit, the more body parts there are that are involved in this movement . . . Our analyses confirmed Condon and Ogston's finding that changes in the patterning of movement which occurs as the subject is speaking are coordinated with changes in the pattern of sound.

(Kendon 1972, p. 205)

William Condon, Albert Scheflen and Adam Kendon are part of an important tradition. A tradition which recognized the interdependence of speech and nonverbal behaviour instead of trying arbitrarily to separate them before despatching them to different disciplines. The research to be reported in this book could be seen to fall into this tradition. However, it is important at the outset to mention that there are a number of methodological problems with the research just reported. McDowall, in an investigation reported in 1978, called the whole phenomenon of interactional synchrony into question on methodological grounds. He had two principal objections. The first one concerned reliability of measurement. He argued that reliability was low for the very fine-grain measurements of the boundaries of movements necessary for the kind of work that Condon and Ogston carried out. His second objection was that chance probability was not taken into account. If several people are engaged in a conversation, one would expect statistically that some of their boundaries of movement would coincide by chance alone. In a study which he carried out of a six person discussion group, he did not find any real evidence of interactional synchrony at an above chance level. This led him to doubt the existence of interactional synchrony. Of course, it could be argued that six first-year students in the laboratory (some unacquainted) might not be relaxed enough to show interactional synchrony, especially since they knew that filming was taking place. Nevertheless, the McDowall study must plant the seeds of doubt in our minds, especially since Condon and Ogston seemed to ignore certain basic methodological principles (that is to say – computing inter-observer reliabilities, or percentage agreement between observers, or computing chance probabilities for the co-occurrences of actions). Similarly, Scheflen and Kendon fail to report inter-observer reliabilities in their studies; instead we just get the reports of these expert observers on behaviour. Furthermore, Scheflen tells us that people show postural congruence when arguing whereas Charny (1966) found that congruence between a therapist and patient was much more likely when the verbal channel also indicated rapport. Charny's findings seem to go directly against Scheflen's observations and it is difficult to decide between them because of the methodological inadequacies. Kendon in his study used a single subject and did not show that any effects generalized across subjects. In addition he used a somewhat vague and idiosyncratic system for the analysis of language (e.g. is a complete sentence not separated by a pause from any preceeding locution *not* a locution and if not, what is it? What does he mean by a distinct pause? The perceptual thresholds of pauses in speech depend critically upon their linguistic location. Is this to be taken into account in the definition?).

The work of Condon, Scheflen and Kendon is too important to be weakened by methodological problems which, when pointed out, can call the phenomena they identified into question. These social scientists pointed to the fundamental organization of language and nonverbal behaviour in conversation. The research reported in this book takes up the challenge of trying to advance these analyses and considerations further whilst at the same time attempting to come to grips with many of the methodological pitfalls that can dog this particular area of research. We now turn immediately to some of the core methodological considerations.

2

Methodological Considerations

A stander-by may sometimes, perhaps, see more of the game than he that plays it.

JONATHAN SWIFT
'A Critical Essay upon the Faculties of the Mind' (1707)

Introduction

This book aims to explore the interconnection between spontaneous speech and nonverbal behaviour in natural conversations. Its goals will have something in common with some of the goals of traditional linguistics (interested in the structure of language), psychology (interested in the structure of nonverbal behaviour) and ethnomethodology (interested in the structure of conversation). Its goals may to some extent be common to all three disciplines, its method, however, will be somewhat distinctive. It will aim to combine the rigour of good psychological research with the breadth of scope of good linguistic and ethnomethodological research.

In chapter 1 I discussed some of the previous research into the relationship between language and nonverbal behaviour. The work of Condon and Ogston (1966, 1967), Scheflen (1964, 1965) and Kendon (1967, 1972) was insightful but so often when reading such research, doubts spring to mind – doubts which could be allayed by greater methodological rigour. A principal consideration in the analysis of behaviour must be the question of reliability, that is, for any categorization scheme to be useful, independent observers should be able to agree on the categorizations of behaviours made (inter-observer reliability) and observers should be able to agree with themselves at a later point in time (test-retest reliability). Any categorization scheme which does not allow independent observers to reach agreement, or which forces an observer into inconsistent decisions at different points in time, is obviously not very useful. Unfortunately, in some of the early core investigations of language and nonverbal behaviour, the issue of reliability was allowed to slip from view. These studies were often brilliant in terms of their conceptual content but left themselves in an extremely vulnerable position on methodological grounds. (Of course, in numerous studies of discourse in linguistics, and in the studies of conversation by ethnomethodologists, the question of reliability has never been raised!) Psychologists have traditionally been those who have treated this issue more seriously and in this book reliability of measurement will come to the fore. Whether it be an analytic scheme for analysing speaker eye-gaze or a descriptive scheme for categorizing interruptions, reliability will be measured and reported for it is the author's basic belief that without satisfactory reliabilities in the analysis, no real progress will be made in the description of behaviour. An emphasis on reliability in measurement will be one main feature of this book.

Another main feature will be the emphasis on the use of statistical techniques, both descriptive and inferential. The majority of the inferential statistics employed will be non-parametric in nature because of the small numbers of subjects used in intensive investigations of this kind and the fact that we can make few assumptions about the underlying distributions of the data. Again, traditionally, statistics have played a much more prominent role in psychology than in linguistics or ethnomethodology. (where they seem to play no role at all.) The basic plan for the description and analysis of behaviour in the conversations studied is to discover tendencies and patterns which are realized throughout the data rather than simply selecting chunks or bits of behaviour which illustrate certain points (as is done in ethnomethodology). The quest for tendencies and patterns will be facilitated by, nay will certainly depend upon, the use of inferential statistics. Statistics will play a prominent role in this book. The outcome of statistical tests will be reported as will the confidence levels for the rejection of any null hypotheses. These statistics will appear frequently in the text and they are to be understood as a metalanguage which both indicates the confidence which I have in the accompanying statements *and* which also tell the reader where the statements derive from. For those non-psychologists who *may* be less familiar with reading this metalanguage, it is worth their perseverence. If one is interested in simplifying and analysing a complete set of data rather than simply searching for and finding specific examples of interesting phenomena, statistics become a necessary tool.

Another basic methodological principle underpinning the research is that single case studies will not be employed (unlike, say, in Kendon 1972). Single case studies have too many potential drawbacks. There is always the danger of ending up with an idiosyncratic subject, an idiosyncratic situation, or both. In this book there will always be some sampling of subjects and any effects identified and reported should generalize across subjects. Any inability to generalize would be considered as a basic problem at some stage in the analysis.

Another guiding principle is that, where possible, the people engaged in conversation will be interfered with as little as possible and the conversations will be as natural as possible. In this book we will concentrate upon tutorials and seminars (recorded at the Universities of Cambridge and Sheffield) with subjects' permission, telephone conversations of the directory enquiry kind recorded by the Post Office, and televised political interviews recorded off the air but watched by several million people in addition to the author. All of these types of conversation are natural in that they would have occurred whether the author had been interested in recording them or not. As such, they are akin to the types of data typically employed by linguists and ethnomethodologists. Psychologists have a rather poorer record here – often using contrived conversational material. (The 'typical' telephone conversation studied by psychologists is two undergraduates in the laboratory with a handset each.) In this series of investigations, the aim was to combine natural samples of behaviour (tutorials are after all one of the few types of conversation which occur naturally in a psychology building), as employed by linguists and ethnomethodologists, together with a certain rigour of analysis that is traditionally found in psychology but sometimes neglected by linguists and ethnomethodologists.

In order to analyse the connections between speech and nonverbal behaviour, it is necessary to look at the behaviour again and again, slow it down, stop it and sometimes even speed it up. This is necessary to unravel the multifarious connections. Video-recording thus presents itself as the obvious way of obtaining samples of behaviour with which one can carry out these operations. Video-recording is cheap, immediate and practical. Some video-recording machines allow one to freeze individual frames and wind on frame-by-frame – these may prove critical facilities in some of the analyses to follow. Video-recorded samples of behaviour allow the investigator to concentrate on the language, the behaviour and the connections between the two. The practicality and necessity of video-recording will be obvious as we go through the individual investigations.

But once we decide on a technique like video-recording, a host of related questions present themselves to us. Where should we position the cameras? Can we get more reliable and valid measures of behaviour when the cameras are out of sight and therefore less obtrusive? Can we use a pair of cameras with a split screen and thereby get records of both partners' behaviour in a conversation or by employing such a procedure do we necessarily diminish the accuracy of measurement? The problem here was that no one had directly confronted these questions before. A number of different practical arrangements had been used for video-recording conversations but no one had tested whether they allowed reasonable levels of reliability or validity in measurement. A first step in the research programme was therefore to test this experimentally using gaze direction – a notoriously difficult behaviour to analyse (see Argyle and Cook 1976, Chapter 2), as the test case.

Analysis of gaze direction

The questions posed here are comparatively simple – can observers accurately judge the direction of gaze of participants engaged in conversation from a video-recording? And secondly, are some practical set ups for video-recording a conversation better than others? Are some of the less obtrusive techniques any good at all?

Rather surprisingly, only one study had investigated whether video-recording could usefully be employed in the analysis of eye-gaze – Rimé and McCusker (1976) compared the accuracy of gaze measurement simultaneously performed by the receiver himself, by a direct-sight observer, by an observer behind a one-way mirror and by an observer using video-recording and viewing the sender's face on a video monitor. They found that an observer using a video-recording technique is able to detect eye-gaze as accurately as the gaze receiver himself, and is more accurate than an observer behind a one-way mirror. This experiment vindicates video-recording but does not tell us which specific techniques for video-recording gaze are the most accurate (Rimé and McCusker used only one technique, with a camera directly pointed at the gaze sender). A number of different techniques have, however, been used in investigations of gaze in dyadic interaction. Some studies have used only one camera behind an interactant to give a full-face view of the other person's face (e.g.

Rutter and Stephenson 1972). Others have analysed the gaze of both interactants and have employed a split screen to combine the input from two cameras situated behind the interactants, each therefore carrying a full-face view (Hedge, Everitt and Frith 1978). Yet other studies have used two cameras and a split screen, but with the cameras behind a one-way mirror or screen and therefore at an angle to the line of regard of the interactants (Stephenson, Rutter and Dore 1973). Duncan (1972), on the other hand, used a single camera with a wide-angle lens for recording the dyadic interactions analysed in his studies (although in these studies he simply analysed head direction rather than gaze). Duncan and Fiske (1977) again used a single camera, this time to analyse gaze. Similarly, Natale (1976) used a single camera with zoom lens at 90° to the sender—receiver axis to analyse gaze patterns. These different techniques vary somewhat in convenience — it is generally most convenient to use cameras behind a one-way mirror, rather than directly behind the interactants. The following study, however (from Beattie and Bogle 1982), seeks to determine whether these different techniques allow reliable and valid measurements of eye-gaze.

METHOD

Recording

Apparatus. Two ITC link cameras and a Sony high-density video-recorder were used to record the interactions.

Procedure. Two subjects sitting five feet apart acted as target gaze-senders. One was male and one was female. They were instructed to change their eye-directed gaze at the onset of a particular auditory signal. The subjects were told that during the periods of no-gaze they could look anywhere except at their partner's eyes (following Rimé and McCusker 1976) but avoid gaze at parts of their interlocutor's face other than their eyes (Argyle 1970). The parameters of programmed gaze were calculated on the basis of natural gaze (Argyle and Cook 1976; Beattie 1978b). There were three gaze conditions: low gaze — the gaze-senders looked at their interlocutor a mean of 35% of the time; medium gaze — approximately 50% of the time; and high gaze — approximately 60% of the time. Nielsen (1962) had reported that the average amount of time spent looking in conversation was 50%. He also found that the average amount of time spent looking while talking was 38%, and while listening — 62%. Thus the three gaze conditions represented in this study reflect the kinds of variation found in natural settings. The auditory signals determining gaze direction were recorded onto the videotapes. Nine different video-recordings were made – three different techniques were used to record the three gaze conditions. Each recording lasted 150 seconds.

Technique A: One camera fitted with a wide-angle lens at 90° to the sender–receiver axis (cf. Duncan 1972; Natale 1976).

Technique B: Two cameras fitted with zoom lens and a split screen. Subjects were filmed by cameras situated behind a one-way mirror so that close-up shots of both subjects (head and shoulders only) orientated towards one another were combined in one picture (as in Stephenson *et al.* 1973).

Technique C: Two cameras fitted with zoom lens and a split screen. Subjects were recorded this time with a camera behind each interactant so that a full-face view was obtained (cf. Hedge *et al.* 1978).

ANALYSIS

Gaze observers. Twelve observers were used. Four male and eight female. All were undergraduates at the University of Sheffield. They analysed the films in six pairs, one member of each pair being assigned to analyse the gaze-behaviour of one of the two target gaze-senders.

Apparatus. A Sony video-recorder and monitor were used to play back the videotapes, and a four-track Rustrak event recorder was used to record the observers' judgements.

PROCEDURE.

Each pair of observers saw all nine films, without sound, in a random order. Each time an observer decided that there was eye-directed gaze from the target gaze-senders they depressed a button to activate the corresponding channel of an event recorder. When they decided that the target gaze-senders were not showing eye-directed gaze they released the button. Using the millimetre scale of the recording chart, it was possible to evaluated by steps of 500 milliseconds the agreement between the records of the observers and those of the corresponding gaze programmes directed by the auditory signals. Validity in gaze measurement was calculated by comparing the observers' responses in each 500 milliseconds time interval, with the auditory signals directing eye-gaze. Reliability, defined as percentage agreement between pairs of observers in gaze judgement in each of the 300 time intervals of 500 milliseconds, was also calculated.

RESULTS

Reliability
There were twelve judges, six observing the male target gaze-sender, and six observing the female target gaze-sender. The percentage agreement between three pairs of judges for each target was thus calculated. Table 2.1 shows the mean reliability or mean percentage agreement between six pairs of judges (averaging across the male and female targets). The overall mean reliability was 75.0%. Given that there were several pairs of judges contributing to this mean (six pairs: twelve judges in all), the effective reliability is even higher (Rosenthal 1979) — the effective reliability can be calculated from the Spearman—Brown formula (Rosenthal 1979):

$$R = \frac{nr}{1 + (n - 1)r}$$ where R = effective reliability and r = mean reliability

The effectiveness reliability would thus seem to be in the region of 0.95. An analysis of variance (ANOVA) was used to compare the effect on reliability ($F = 8.853$, d.f. = 2, 8, $p < 0.01$). Technique C between pairs of judges. Video-recording technique had a significant effect on reliability ($f = 8.853$, d.f. = 2, 8, $p < 0.01$). Technique C allowed greatest reliability — 81.5%, compared with 69.9% for technique A. Level of gaze did not significantly affect reliability ($F = 1.859$, d.f. = 2, 8, n.s.). There was, however, a significant interaction effect between recording technique and gaze level ($F = 4.054$, d.f. = 4, 16, $p < 0.02$). In the case of technique C, judges were most reliable with a low level of gaze, and similarly with A. But with technique B, judges were most reliable with a medium level of gaze. The specific target gaze-sender did not significantly affect reliability ($F = 0.273$, d.f. = 1, 4, n.s.); neither were there any

Table 2.1 Reliability of different video-recording techniques (mean percentage agreement between judges)

| Gaze level | Video-recording technique | | | Means |
	A	B	C	
Low	72.9	69.4	86.0	76.1
Medium	65.7	85.7	82.1	77.8
High	71.0	65.9	76.5	71.1
Means	69.9	73.7	81.5	Grand mean 75.0

Table 2.2 Validity of different video-recording techniques (mean percentage correct gaze judgements)

Gaze level	Video-recording technique			Means
	A	B	C	
Low	72.9	73.9	78.4	75.1
Medium	69.4	67.1	81.9	72.8
High	69.2	67.2	72.1	69.5
Means	70.5	69.4	77.5	Grand mean 72.5

significant interaction effects between target gaze-sender and video-recording technique or level of gaze.

Validity

The overall mean percentage correct gaze judgement was found to be 72.5% (see Table 2.2). An ANOVA revealed that video-recording technique significantly affected validity of gaze measurement ($F = 7.646$, d.f. $= 2, 20, p < 0.01$). Video-recording technique C allowed greatest accuracy in gaze measurement (mean accuracy 77.5%). There was little difference in accuracy using techniques A and B (mean accuracy score for A, 70.5% and for B, 69.4%). The effects of level of gaze on validity of gaze measurement failed to reach significance ($F = 2.95$, d.f. $= 2, 20$, n.s.). The interaction effect between video-recording technique and gaze level also failed to reach significance ($F = 2,190$, d.f. $= 4, 40$, n.s.). The specific target gaze-sender did not significantly affect validity of gaze measurement ($F = 1.089$, d.f. $= 1, 10$, n.s.).

CONCLUSION

In this investigation I explicitly raised the question of whether video-recording allows reliable and valid measurement of eye-gaze – a central component of nonverbal communication and one dealt with in detail in this book. The answer was an unequivocal 'yes'. Overall, the effective reliability of using video-recording for analysing eye-gaze was 95% with an average validity of 72.5%. There were significant differences in both reliability and validity for different techniques. The set up with two cameras and a split screen with the cameras behind each interactant so that a full-face view of each person appears on the video monitor was superior to other techniques. But nevertheless the two other techniques tested did allow measurement of eye-gaze at a high and certainly acceptable level of accuracy.

And since these two techniques — a camera with a wide-angle lens at 90° to the sender—receiver axis (cf. Duncan 1972), and two cameras with zoom lenses and a split screen but behind a one-way mirror (cf. Stephenson *et al.* 1973) were less obtrusive than the other technique; these were the techniques actually employed in this research programme.

Pause analysis

As in the case of the nonverbal components of behaviour, the emphasis in the analysis of speech was on objectivity, reliability and validity. This was especially the case in the analysis of the temporal aspects of speech. As Goldman-Eisler (1968) said:

> Somehow the phenomenon of speech has become associated with images which suggest continuity in sound production. We speak of the even flow, of fluency in speech, of a flood of language and many words relating to speech derive from descriptions of water in motion, such as 'gush, spout, stream, torrent of speech, floodgates of speech etc.'
> The facts, however, show these images to be illusory; if we measure vocal continuity by the number of words uttered between two pauses, and call "phrase" the sequence uttered without break, we obtain a picture of fragmentation rather than of continuity . . . 50% of (unprepared) speech is broken up into phrases of less than three words . . . 90% less than ten words (p. 17).

> Spontaneous speech was shown to be a highly fragmented and discontinuous activity. When even at its most fluent, two-thirds of spoken language comes in chunks of less than six words, the attribute of flow and fluency in spontaneous speech must be judged an illusion (p. 31).

Frieda Goldman-Eisler's striking conclusions derived from her pioneering studies of spontaneous speech. She was concerned with an objective record of spontaneous speech, not what speaker-hearers, i.e. conversationalists, noticed or said or perceived. Her studies of spontaneous speech were based on an objective analysis of any pauses in speech exceeding 250 milliseconds. (She needed to employ some temporal criterion in order to exclude discontinuities of phonation which occur in articulatory shifts, e.g. when two plosives or stops follow each other, as in top part, tat, tat; see Goldman-Eisler 1968, p. 12.) In a series of studies she demonstrated that these objectively measurable silences in speech played a crucial role in the planning of spontaneous speech at both the lexical and semantic level.

The research methodology concerning pauses in speech in this book was based on Frieda Goldman-Eisler's pioneering work. Pauses in speech were objectively measured using, in the earliest research, the Ediswan pen oscillograph employed by Goldman-Eisler. This device operates on the principle that an output from a tape recorder or video-recorder is fed through a signal detector which translates the signal into pulses coextensive in time with the duration of the speech periods.

> This in turn is fed into a pen oscillograph. The pen recorder is set so as to make pauses apparent down to a length of one-tenth of a second – which is more than sufficiently accurate for showing up pauses relevant to output of words. (See Goldman-Eisler 1968, p. 11)

The only change made from Goldman-Eisler's work was that the minimal criterial definition of a pause was lowered from 250 milliseconds to 200 milliseconds (following Boomer 1965). In some of the later studies a 'pauseometer' which operated on a very similar principle was employed. The operation of the pauseometer is as follows.

The recorded audio signal is first amplified and full-wave rectified. The rectified output passes through a low-pass filter with a time constant of 33 milliseconds. The output from the filter represents the speech intensity 'envelope'. This signal is then compared with a fixed reference voltage giving a digital speech/pause output signal. In use, the gain of the amplifier stage is adjusted to be as high as possible without producing spurious 'speech' outputs from the background noise level. The measured response time of the pauseometer over the audio frequency range 150 Hz to 20 kHz is 10 milliseconds for a pause-to-speech transition and 40–60 milliseconds for a speech-to-pause transition. These measurements were made with a sinusoidal tone-burst input and so probably represent worst-case figures.

In the present series of studies, objective temporal measurement was made both in the case of pauses within a speaker-turn, which Goldman-Eisler had concentrated on, as well as pauses between turns in conversation – so-called 'switching-pauses' (see Jaffe and Feldstein 1970). This methodology differs considerably from that employed by ethnomethodologists interested in conversational analysis. Zimmerman and West (1975), for example, describe their method for analysing the duration of switching pauses as follows:

> Silences between utterances were timed by stop watch twice and averaged (p. 113).

Within-turn pauses are similarly analysed in the ethnomethodological framework. Such procedures obviously depend upon observers perceiving the pause in the first instance because if they do not perceive it, presumably they cannot even begin to time it with a stop watch (not considering for the moment the problems inherent in using a stop watch to time short but perhaps highly significant pauses). However, Martin (1970) has provided conclusive evidence that observers often do not hear certain pauses in speech. He found that in a speech corpus involving 183 objective silences, the observers failed to detect 33 of them — that is 18% of the total. But in addition they 'detected' 23 that were not actually present. Martin identified the intonation features which seemed to affect pause judgements.

> When scorers judged a pause where there was no measured silent interval, the last syllable of the word preceding the pause was longer than the first syllable of the following word in nearly every case. When there was a silent interval, there was usually an elongated syllable prior to the pause interval. When, however, the machine detected a silent interval but the scorers did not, the syllable following the interval was usually longer. It does appear that elongated syllables at the end of a word may serve as a cue for pause judgements.
>
> (Martin 1970, p. 63)

Martin's findings would suggest that any research strategy which uses observer's perceptions of pause patterns will not yield valid measurements of actual pauses present in speech. Goldman-Eisler's work, however, did suggest that it was indeed these objective silences, often of very short durations, which were functionally important for the generation of spontaneous speech. The present research follows the Goldman-Eisler example and aims to provide an objective, reliable and valid account of the temporal organization of speech in conversation.

Transcription

It has become clear in recent years that for transcription purposes, the audio channel alone can yield a vast amount of data. It seems to be widely accepted that when video-recording is employed for data collection, the amount of potential material can simply be too vast to handle. The primary motivation guiding transcription in the observational studies of conversation in this book was not to attempt to represent everything, for that would be impossible, or indeed everything that could potentially be important with respect to the prime research considerations. Rather, selective features were identified and transcribed in detail — first all words were transcribed and then all unfilled pauses $\geq$ 200 milliseconds, (measured with the appropriate device) and all filled hesitations were analyzed and marked on the verbal transcript. Filled hesitations consist of the four subcategories defined as follows:

Repetitions. All repetitions, of any length, that were judged to be non-significant semantically.

Parenthetic remarks. Words and phrases like 'I mean', 'sort of', 'well', 'you know' that seem irrelevant to semantic communication.

Filled pauses. Ah, er, um, etc.

False starts. All incomplete or self-interrupted utterances, plus speech errors which were subsequently corrected. False starts are *in italics* in the following examples:

> 'But um *the idea that* um I suppose that the idea is that they deserve it' (filled pauses: 2; false starts: 3).
> '*You go you turn outsi* − you go outside the front door and you turn *left* sorry right' (false starts: 6).
> 'She might *have alre* − have a lot of children already and *can't feel* feels that she can't provide for *the child* an extra child' (false starts: 7).

The features identified are those most closely associated with planning aspects of spontaneous speech. In addition, all simultaneous speech was transcribed and the duration of each individual 'switching-pause' (pause between speaker-turns) was measured using the pauseometer and marked on the transcripts. These features again are identified from the audio channel but these of course have most direct bearing on structural features of conversation. In the visual channel the prime focus was on patterns of speaker eye-gaze and gesture. Using the slow-motion facility on the video edit machine, the precise time of each eye-gaze by the speaker at the listener was noted and mapped onto the transcript. When speakers closed their eyes or averted eye-gaze, this was also noted. In the case of gestures, the time of the initiation and termination of each movement was noted and again mapped onto the transcript. In addition to a verbal transcript, what might be called a temporal transcript was also made − the pattern of unfilled pauses and bursts of phonation was plotted across time. Also, the position of each pause within a speaker-turn was marked on the verbal transcript, and its length measured and noted. The initiation and termination of each speaker gaze at the listener and each speaker gesture was mapped onto the temporal transcript as well.

This chapter has set out the general methodological context for the exploration of talk. Naturally and necessarily each of the following chapters will embody, qualify and expand this context.

3

The temporal structure of spontaneous speech

It's alright to hesitate if you then go ahead.

BERTOLT BRECHT
'The Good Woman of Setzuan'(1938–40)

Introduction

In the next two chapters we begin the exploration of the relationship between language and nonverbal behaviour. By 'language' here we mean speech — spontaneous speech as it is produced for the first time, in this particular case, within the context of a conversation. The conversations are tutorials and seminars, the tutorials here being dyadic, i.e. two-party interactions. These are very special kinds of conversation, of course, but they do nevertheless involve linguistic encoding, the behaviours like eye-gaze and gesture which may be connected to linguistic encoding, listener feedback, turn-taking (even if asymmetrically distributed across the participants — tutors are notoriously loquacious!) and a good deal of cognition and behaviour coming together generally. The social aspects of interaction may be somewhat restricted here — tutorials are often low on the communication of affect for instance. But in an exploratory study of this kind, this may be an advantage. The method of analysis should be capable of being generalized to much more 'social' contexts. The analysis of language will differ markedly from those analyses presented by Condon and Ogston (1966, 1967), Scheflen (1964, 1965) and Kendon (1972). The focus here will be on the units of planning and production of spontaneous speech — so-called encoding units (see Lounsbury 1954): units with demonstrable psycholinguistic reality and not merely useful descriptive units in the analysis of language. The emphasis throughout is on spontaneous speech rather than any other forms of language.

Encoding units in spontaneous speech

Spontaneous speech is unlike written text. It contains many mistakes, sentences are usually brief and indeed the whole fabric of verbal expression is riddled with hesitations and silences. To take a very simple example: in a seminar which I recorded, an articulate (and well-known) linguist was attempting to say the following:

> No, I'm coming back to the judgements question. Indeterminacy appears to be rife. I don't think it is, if one sorts out which are counterexamples to judgement.

But what he actually said was:

> No *I'm saying* I'm coming back to the judgements question (267) *you know there appear to* (200) *ah* indeterminacy (1467) appears to be rife. I don't think it is (200) *if one* (267) if one sorts out which are counterexamples (267) to judgement, *I mean observing*.

Here, the brief silences (unfilled pauses) have been measured in milliseconds and marked (these are the numbers in brackets) and all other types of hesitation — false starts, repetitions, filled pauses and parenthetic remarks put in italics. It is these hesitations (both filled and unfilled) which dominate spontaneous speech and give it its distinctive structure and feeling. In this chapter we explore in detail what these hesitations reveal about the nature of units in spontaneous speech. It should be explained at the outset that unfilled pauses take up a considerable amount of time in speech. Goldman-Eisler (1968), for example, found that:

> Interviews of eight subjects lasting thirty minutes to an hour showed that the mean proportions of utterance time taken up by pauses ranged between 4% and 54%. Even the more fluent speakers among these subjects (whose pause time proportion was less than 30%) produced on occasion utterances in which time was more than equally balanced between pausing and speaking . . . Discussions on various selected subjects showed a similar spread between 13% and 63% and impromptu talks on selected topics produced pause time proportions of between 35% and 67%.

A similar picture was obtained from spontaneous speech uttered in response to a request to describe picture stories . . . Again we have a wide variation from 16% to 62% of utterance time spent in silence. Most of the group, however, paused between 40% and 50% of their total speaking time. These values seem to be ample evidence that pausing is as much part of speech as vocal utterance.

(p. 18)

The function of these many silent periods seem to be the planning of spontaneous speech (see Rochester 1973). Goldman-Eisler (1968) devised a series of tasks which involved subjects either describing or interpreting cartoons from the *New Yorker*. Subjects had to then repeat their description or interpretation in an attempt to investigate the relationship between spontaneity and amount of pausing in speech. Goldman-Eisler's results were quite striking.

The results showed that pausing time when speakers interpreted meaning was about twice as much as when they described content. Pausing also varied with the different degrees of spontaneity. There was a sudden decline after the first trial and a gradual decrease of pausing in the subsequent repetitions. This was taken to indicate that the difference between spontaneity and reiteration, between production and reproduction, is a qualitative one, reflecting the dual nature of psycholinguistic operations.

(Goldman-Eisler 1968, p. 59)

It has been suggested that hesitations are in fact an integral and necessary part of spontaneous speech. The principle form of hesitation as we have already discussed, is the unfilled pause − any period of silence in speech over a certain minimal criterion (usually 200 milliseconds). Other forms of hesitation include filled pauses, repetitions that are not semantically significant, false starts or self-corrected utterances, and parenthetic remarks which can often convey little of any semantic worth (see also Goffman 1981). Pauses may be integral to speech in terms of their widespread annd persistent nature, but are they also integral to speech in the sense that spontaneous speech cannot occur without them? Do we really need to pause in order to speak coherently and sensibly? This was tested in an experiment I carried out with Ros Bradbury (Beattie and Bradbury 1979). We set up an operant conditioning procedure to attempt to change the frequency of pauses in speech − subjects told stories and we made the onset of a light contingent upon pauses of a certain duration (600 milliseconds). In one condition it was explained to subjects that the light was going to be used to signal that their story-telling was particularly poor at certain points (but of course the light was simply affected by the presence of pauses). But did this 'punishment' contingency reduce the number of pauses in speech as subjects attempted to improve their apparently poor story-telling performance as signalled by the light? The answer seemed to be yes. The number of 600 millisecond pauses was in fact reduced by 35% but this reduction was accompanied by a large and dramatic increase in the amount of repetition in speech — subjects began repeating syllables and words, even whole phrases to a much greater extent. In the final 'punishment' trial, the amount of repetition was up by a factor of 104% compared with the baseline trials (see also Beattie 1979d). In other words, *hesitations* would seem to be an integral part of speech in every sense — subjects cannot produce spontaneous speech without them, although speakers do seem to be able to substitute repetition in speech for unfilled pauses, when required. It should also be added that this whole change in behaviour seemed to occur in the absence of the conscious knowledge of the subjects concerned. Some subjects noticed that the light indicating poor performance came on when they were not saying anything but they explained this to the experimenter afterwards by suggesting that the light was referring to something they had said before the gap in the speech!

If pauses and hesitations are necessary for planning spontaneous speech, then they would seem to offer themselves as useful and important tools to those interested in the patterning of the psycholinguistic processes underlying the generation of spontaneous speech.

Lounsbury (1954, p. 100) was the first to hypothesize that the distribution of hesitations in speech might reveal something about the nature of encoding units in spontaneous speech:

> Hesitation pauses and points of high statistical uncertainty correspond to the beginnings of units of encoding.

He was operating with a fairly simplistic model of language which was to be understood in terms of the statistical tendencies between certain words occurring in spontaneous speech. Hesitation pauses were hypothesized to occur before the most unpredictable words which reflected the cognitive planning of the speaker. Predictable expressions such as clichés required much less planning. An examination of where hesitations occur should thus tell us something about the distribution of the speaker's planning processes. The earliest experimental studies testing this hypothesis focussed on encoding units at the word level and a significant relationship between hesitations and words of relatively low transitional probability, as measured by the Shannon guessing technique, was reported by Goldman-Eisler (1958a, 1958b). The Shannon guessing technique involves subjects guessing each successive word in a sentence. To put it simply, the more difficult a word is to guess, the more unpredictable it is. Thus if I have a certain sentence in mind and I ask the reader to guess the sentence, the reader might suggest 'The' as the first word. This would be correct. The second word would probably be the most difficult to guess: 'boy?', 'girl?', 'bus?', 'hammer?', 'man?', 'knife?', 'dog?'. 'Dog' is correct. The third would probably be much easier: 'sat?', 'bit?'. Correct. The fourth would be easier still: 'the?'. Correct. The fifth would be more difficult: 'cat?', 'boy?', 'postman?', 'woman?', 'girl?', 'man?', 'work-man?'. Correct. The more difficult the word is to guess, the lower is its transitional probability. Goldman-Eisler found that pauses preceded the words of lowest transitional probability. In the hypothetical sentence above the pause would probably precede 'dog'.

However, these studies have subsequently been criticized both for their use of an unrepresentative sample of speech, and for their dubious statistical analysis (Boomer 1970). The speech sample was unrepresentative because it consisted of twelve sentences – only 'grammatically correct . . . well constructed sentences . . . logically consistent with the whole utterance' were considered (see Goldman-Eisler 1968, p. 36). In 'grammatically correct . . . well constructed' sentences, words are obviously much easier to guess than in ungrammatical sentences. It would be interesting to see if the same relationship held for ungrammatical speech. Furthermore, in an investigation I carried out with Brian Butterworth (Beattie and Butterworth 1979), we demonstrated that the 'guessability' of words in text is often confounded with their individual frequency in the language as a whole. Infrequent words are, generally speaking, more difficult to guess and therefore more unpredictable than frequent words, and therefore a speaker's having to search the mental lexicon for words of low frequency could partly account for the fact that pauses precede unpredictable words. (See also Oldfield and Wingfield 1965; Taylor 1969; Mercer 1976).

Other evidence has suggested that the typical encoding unit is somewhat larger than the word. Maclay and Osgood (1959) observed that false starts, where a speaker starts an utterance, stops abruptly and re-starts, usually involve not just corrections of the unintended word, but also corrections of the associated function words (such as 'the'). Boomer (1965) analysed the distribution of hesitations with respect to phonemic clauses (the formal definition of which is 'phonologically marked macrosegments containing one, and only one, primary stress, and ending in one of the terminal junctures /I, II, III/' (Trager and Smith 1951) – basically units involving one main stress), and observed that both unfilled pauses (UPs) and filled pauses (FPs: 'ah', 'er', 'um', etc.) tended to occur towards the beginnings of such clauses. He thus concluded that 'planning ranges forward to encompass a structured chunk of syntax and meaning' (Boomer 1965, p. 91), where such chunks were thought to correspond to these so-called 'phonemic clauses'. However, the modal position of hesitations (i.e. the most frequent position of hesitations) was found to be between the first and second word of the clause, and not before the first word, as expected. This result has been given a number of interpretations. Barik (1968) argued that Boomer's decision to regard all UPs at clause junctures (unless accompanied by an FP or word fragment) as being simply linguistically determined because they are at grammatically appropriate locations, was too conservative, and he hypothesized that long juncture pauses (i.e. UPs > 500 milliseconds) have a cognitive as well as a purely linguistic function. Such long pauses, he argued, would surely not be necessary to demarcate clausal units. If one accepts Barik's suggestion that long pauses at clause junctures probably have a cognitive as well as a linguistic function, the modal position of hesitations shifts to before the first word of the clause. An alternative interpretation has suggested that the modal position of hesitations is as observed by Boomer because a new syntactic clause is often introduced at this point. (See Fodor *et al.* 1974; p. 424.) This interpretation suggests that the syntactic clause is the basic unit of encoding. There is evidence from another source to support this hypothesis. Valian (1971) used reaction times to assess the processing load of speakers on the assumption that the less a speaker is doing cognitively, the faster should be his or her reaction to an extraneous stimulus, such as a randomly generated tone. Valian, in fact, found that speakers' reaction times to randomly generated tones were significantly faster when the tone occurred on the last, rather than the first word of syntactic clauses in their speech. This suggests that the speaker is engaged in less processing towards the end of a clause than at the beginning, which of course would be predicted by a clausal model. However, since syntactic clauses do not invariably begin after the first word of a phonemic clause (Fodor *et al.* 1974, p. 422) any conclusion from the Boomer (1965) data on syntactic clauses must be tentatively drawn. For stronger support, the analysis of hesitations must be performed with respect to syntactic clauses.

A number of other studies have found that if the durations of individual pause and phonation periods in speech are measured and graphically represented, then, when lines are fitted to represent changes in relative fluency, a cyclic pattern of relatively steep slopes (high pause/phonation ratio) alternating with relatively shallow slopes (low pause/phonation ratio) appears in samples of spontaneous speech, but *not* in those of prose readings. In other words, spontaneous speech does not display a fixed amount of hesitancy per unit time (but see Jaffe *et al.* 1972). Moreover, it has been observed that the fluent phases of these cycles are characterized by fewer filled hesitations (FPs, repetitions and false starts) and by a higher proportion of pauses at grammatical junctures. The amount of pausing in the hesitant phase of these cycles has also been found to be directly related to the amount of phonation in the succeeding fluent phase. It has' thus been hypothesized that the fluent phases are planned in the preceding hesitant phases (Henderson *et al.* 1966; Goldman-Eisler 1967). A hesitant phase plus the succeeeding fluent phase has been termed a 'temporal cycle'. The duration of these temporal cycles has been found to range between 10.6 and 39.3 seconds, with a mean of 18.0 seconds (Butterworth 1975) which suggests that such units are substantially larger than individual clauses which are only a matter of a couple of seconds in duration. These temporal or cognitive cycles have also been found to correspond to 'ideas' as judged by subjects in the speech text (Butterworth 1975). Ideas are, of course, semantic rather than syntactic, and it has been suggested therefore that the main encoding units in spontaneous speech are semantic and not syntactic in nature.

However, because of a number of lacunae in the research, none of these studies can be considered to allow definite conclusions about encoding units in speech. The first lacuna in the research is that no study has successfully accounted for all (or nearly all) the hesitation data. In the Boomer (1965) study, only 54.3% of hesitations could be accounted for by holistic planning of the clause, since 45.7% of hesitations occurred later than the second word of the clause. No attempt was made to determine the function of these residual pauses. Similarly, studies of temporal cycles have found that hesitations, whose function could not be semantic planning, occur in the fluent phases of cycles. Henderson *et al.* (1966) reported that 45.7% of all UPs at nongrammatical junctures occurred in these fluent phases. Butterworth (1976) has suggested that some of these hesitations may be used for lexical selection, and he has in fact shown that approximately 32% of pauses in the fluent phases of cycles precede relatively unpredictable words. The function of the majority of hesitations in fluent phases, however, has still to be elucidated.

The second lacuna in all earlier studies is that inferences about cognitive processes in speech have been made solely on the basis of analyses of hesitations. It is clear, however, that some pauses may have a linguistic or social function, since some (notably UPs at grammatical junctures) occur even in reading (Goldman-Eisler 1972). Other pauses may have less obvious social functions. For example, it has been hypothesized that filled pauses are used in conversation to prevent interruption by the listener (Maclay and Osgood 1959; Beattie 1977). It would clearly be useful to have access to additional information about the nature of cognitive processing in speech. One potential indicator of cognitive activity is the patterning of gaze of a speaker engaged in conversation. Speakers look at listeners for information − to see how they are reacting to what is being said and sometimes perhaps to see if the listener wants the floor (see also Kendon 1967, 1972). This looking may interfere with the cognitive planning underlying speech and indeed there is now substantial evidence to suggest that speakers avert their gaze during planning periods in speech to reduce potential interference. Nielsen (1962) observed that subjects averted gaze when preparing arguments in conversation. Kendon (1967) found that gaze aversion was more likely during slow hesitant speech than during fluent speech. Exline and Winters (1965) found that the overall amount of gaze in conversation was inversely related to the cognitive difficulty of the topic of conversation. Weiner and Ehrlichman (1976) in a re-analysis of the Ehrlichman *et al.* (1974) data, discovered significantly more instances of eye closing when subjects were answering spatial rather than verbal questions (presumably because more interference is likely between the incoming visual information and the imagery processes required in answering spatial questions).

But can we demonstrate experimentally actual interference between a speaker looking at a listener and cognitive planning in spontaneous speech? This is attempted in the following experiment (described also in Beattie 1981a).

Cognitive planning and eye contact

Ehrlichman (1981) attempted the first direct test of the hypothesis that there is interference between cognitive planning in speech and eye contact. He argued that 'In order to conclude that people avert gaze to reduce distraction, it would appear necessary to demonstrate that people would in fact be distracted, if such gaze aversion was not possible'. To this end, Ehrlichman compared response latency (that is the delay in milliseconds before responding), fluency of response (as reflected in mean length of hesitation pause during the subject's verbal response) and judged quality of subjects' answers to questions asked by an interviewer whose face was either visible or not visible on a video-screen. Ehrlichman did not find any evidence of interference during continuous gaze at the face on the video-screen, on any of these measures. Indeed, response latency was shorter when subjects gazed continuously at the face than when gaze was free to vary, contrary to expectations. However, this study cannot be considered a definitive test, for two reasons. Firstly, the face of the interviewer which subjects had to gaze at was not the face of a person actually present but rather a face presented on a video-screen; a real human face may be more distracting because of its greater social presence (see Short *et al.* 1976). There is considerable evidence to suggest that eye contact may lead to increased levels of arousal in subjects. Eye contact initiated by a confederate has been shown to produce increased galvanic skin responses (GSRs) (e.g. Nichols and Champness 1971), increased heart rate (e.g. Kleinke and Pohlen 1971), and decreased electroencephalogram (EEG) activity (e.g. Gale *et al.* 1972). All of these physiological measures have been hypothesized to reflect arousal (see Patterson 1976). A face on a video-screen may be much less arousing, however. Secondly, the measures Ehrlichman made of the speech produced in this experiment may not have been sufficiently sensitive. We do not know, for example, how sensitive his seven-point rating scale of verbal quality of subjects' responses was. No difference in the other two measures taken by Ehrlichman – response latency and verbal fluency – may simply mean that when confronted by a face on a video-screen, subjects respond quickly and fluently but produce much more vocalized hesitation and speech errors. Ehrlichman did not attempt to assess the incidence of vocalized hesitations in his subjects' speech; phenomena like false starts (that is self-corrected utterances), repetitions and filled pauses (ah, er, um, etc.) would have been classified in his experiment as 'fluent speech'. Many of these filled hesitations directly reflect encoding difficulty (see McNeill 1979, chapter 9).

The aim of the following investigation was to examine whether there is a deleterious effect on language production when constant gaze at another person's face is required from someone speaking spontaneously in social interaction.

METHOD

Subjects
Ten undergraduates (eight females, two males) from the University of Sheffield acted as subjects. All were interviewed by the same person – a female undergraduate.

Equipment

Pauseometer. As described in Chapter 2, p. 29.

Computer analysis. The digital speech/pause output of the pauseometer is fed into a Nascom 2 microcomputer and analysed by a simple timing program written in BASIC. The computer automatically measures the durations of the response latency and individual pause and phonation intervals during the selected passage, and displays a separate total for each. (Silences less than 200 milliseconds were not classified as unfilled pauses (following Boomer 1965).)

PROCEDURE

Subjects sat at a distance of five feet from the interviewer. The interviewer asked four questions in random order – two were verbal – linguistic in nature ('Could you outline the arguments for and against (1) abortion, (2) capital punishment?'); and two were visual–spatial in nature (1) 'Could you describe how to get from the Psychology Department to your house in Sheffield?' (2) 'Could you describe your bedroom?'). The interviewer looked downwards at the question sheet while reading the questions to the subjects and looked continuously at her interlocutor until the subject finished the answer. Subjects were instructed to look continuously at the interviewer during their answer to one question of each type. Subjects' gaze behaviour was video-recorded and subsequently analysed to ensure that they complied with this instruction. The natural focus for gaze is at one's interlocutor's eyes. No subjects were observed to display aberrant gaze behaviour in terms of focus of regard. During their answers to the other two questions they were permitted free eye movements. The experiment was video-recorded using Sony high-density equipment by a camera behind a one-way mirror; a microphone was suspended in the room. From the videotape, response latency, total pause time and total speech time were analysed using the pauseometer and Nascom 2 microcomputer. The speech was then transcribed and the number of words counted (can't, don't, etc., were counted as two words). All filled hesitations were then identified and these were again counted in words.

RESULTS

(A Wilcoxon matched-pairs signed-ranks test was used in all comparisons. All probabilities are two-tailed.)
   Analysis revealed that continuous gaze at an interviewer did not

significantly affect response latency, either in the case of answers to verbal–linguistic questions (T = 22, n = 9, p > 0.05) or in the case of answers to visual–spatial questions (T = 23, n = 10, p > 0.05). The means are presented in Table 3.1. Similarly, the effects of looking continuously at the interviewer did not significantly affect speech rate, either in the case of answers to verbal questions (T = 21, n = 10, p > 0.05) or in the case of answers to spatial questions (T = 19½, n = 10, p > 0.05). Also, looking continuously at an interviewer did not significantly affect the other measure of fluency – unfilled pause time per unit speech time – for verbal questions (T = 11½, n = 10, p > 0.05) or for spatial questions (T = 25, n = 10, p > 0.05).

However, some measures of filled hesitation in this study were significantly affected by the gaze manipulation. The composite measure of filled hesitation (corrected for the number of words produced) approximately doubled. It was significantly higher when subjects looked continuously at the interviewer when answering verbal questions (T = 4, n = 10, p < 0.02) and when answering spatial questions (T = 4, n = 10, p < 0.02). Repetitions, parenthetic remarks and filled pauses did not significantly increase under the fixed gaze condition. On the other hand, false starts increased dramatically.

Table 3.1 The effects of continuous gaze at the face of an interviewer on measures of language production

	Normal gaze		Continuous gaze	
Means	*Verbal*	*Spatial*	*Verbal*	*Spatial*
Response latency (s)	0.69	0.65	1.06	0.49
Speech rate (words/min)	128	145	134	135
Unfilled pause time/total speech time	0.373	0.329	0.330	0.328
Filled hesitation rate (per unit word spoken)	0.077	0.050	0.147	0.126
False starts (per unit word spoken)	0.019	0.007	0.077	0.072
Repetitions (per unit word spoken)	0.004	0.005	0.005	0.005
Filled pauses (per unit word spoken)	0.047	0.037	0.052	0.042
Parenthetic remarks (per unit word spoken)	0.007	0.001	0.014	0.008

In the case of spatial questions, false starts increased by a factor of approximately 10 under the condition of continuous gaze at the face. There were significantly more false starts per unit word spoken when looking continuously at the interviewer when answering verbal questions ($T = 0$, $n = 9$, $p < 0.01$) and spatial questions ($T = 0$, $n = 6$, $p < 0.05$).

DISCUSSION

The results obtained here suggest that gaze at the face of another person does significantly interfere with the production of spontaneous speech. Filled hesitations and especially false starts become significantly more common in speech in the condition of continuous gaze at the face of the other person. Ehrlichman's failure to observe an interference effect in a similar situation would seem to critically depend on his decision to employ a face presented on a video-screen rather than a physically present interviewer, and his failure to analyse the speech produced (apart from a rather global rating of quality of answers). When speakers look continuously at an interviewer they begin utterances quickly (as indexed by the response latency), but they often have to retrace their steps. David McNeill (1979), who has described some of the processes of spontaneous language production, would identify such instances as 'build-ups' and 'break-downs'. Speech errors which were subsequently corrected were included as examples of false starts. Subjects often produced a number of inappropriate words before hitting on the correct one. They were also aware of their problem. In one particular room description, a subject who was having a good deal of trouble in finding the right word, when asked to look continuously at the interviewer, volunteered the opinion 'I know, you are trying to prove this is impossible'. Speakers are clearly distracted by having to look continuously at a human face. This study, however, does support Ehrlichman's observation that continuous gaze at a human face does not significantly affect measures of fluency other than filled hesitations. It should be noted, however, that in the present study this manipulation had no significant effect on response latency, whereas Ehrlichman observed a significantly shorter latency when gaze was fixed at a face on a video-screen.

This study has demonstrated that interference does occur, contrary to the evidence of Ehrlichman (1981). It does not, however, pinpoint the mechanism mediating the speech disruption. Argyle and Cook (1976) have attempted to explain the phenomenon in terms of 'cognitive overload', on the assumption that visual monitoring and speech planning peformed simultaneously will exceed some fixed attentional limits. However, recent studies on attention, and specifically on concurrent cognitive tasks, suggest that speakers should be able to manage speech planning and simultaneous visual monitoring (see Allport 1980). Indeed, it has been demonstrated that, *with practice*, subjects can perform a variety of complex cognitive tasks simul taneously without any obvious loss of performance. Spelke *et al.* (1976) demonstrated that, after some weeks of practice, subjects were able to write words at dictation while reading for comprehension at normal speed. Spelke *et al.* conclude: 'The performance of these subjects is not consistent with the notion that there are fixed limits to attentional capacity' (1976, p. 215). Hatano *et al.* (1977) demonstrated that expert abacus operators could answer simple non-mathematical questions during abacus calculation without increasing time or errors. Practice seems to be crucially important to efficient dual-task performance, but as competent conversationalists, we all should have considerable practice at simultaneously monitoring a human face and planning and producing language since the two do occur simultaneously in conversation for at least some proportion of the time. If one sums across the numerous conversations that most of us experience in a lifetime, those small periods of simultaneously monitoring and planning speech add up to considerable dual-task experience.

Given doubts about the 'cognitive overload' hypothesis based on severe attentional limits, an alternative hypothesis would be that the effect is due to arousal. Eye contact may lead to greater levels of emotional arousal in subjects (Kleinke and Pohlen 1971; Nichols and Champness 1971; Patterson 1976) and this increased level of arousal may interfere with the cognitive planning of spontaneous speech. Reynolds and Paivio (1968) demonstrated that a number of measures of language production are affected by emotional arousal. They found that certain hesitation phenomena increased in the speech of subjects high in audience sensitivity when in the presence of an audience. Thus the interference we observed when speakers planned and produced spontaneous speech and looked at their interlocuter could easily have arisen as a function of the arousal caused by the eye contact.

Since interference does occur, speaker eye-gaze offers itself as a useful additional tool in the analysis of planning in spontaneous speech.

Cognitive planning in spontaneous speech

The next step in the research was to analyse the distribution of hesitations in a sample of spontaneous speech but, in addition, to video-record the speaker in action, in order to analyse the patterns of eye-gaze as additional evidence of cognitive processing. The review of the literature on hesitations showed that a number of different models had been proposed − a number of different models which were never tested or resolved. In this investigation, the two competing models − the clausal (Boomer 1965) and supraclausal (Henderson *et al.* 1966) models − are tested in the same set of data with additional analyses of speaker gaze in order to sort out possible sources of confusion, such as the possible cognitive function of pauses at clause junctures. Thus in this investigation, two lines of evidence are brought together to test a number of models of language production.

PROCEDURE

Four interactions were filmed, three were hour-long supervisions involving a teacher and an undergraduate. The remaining sample involved two participants of a seminar, engaged in a prolonged interaction. All speakers analysed were male and only one interaction involved a mixed-sex pair. The supervisions and seminar took place in a comfortable observation room with Sony video cameras located behind a one-way mirror. All subjects were informed that filming was to take place.

The present study concentrated on the speech and gaze of five subjects. The speech samples analysed were randomly selected from the speech corpus, with the constraint that the speaker's turn in conversation had to be at least 30 seconds in length, so that temporal cycles could be identified. The corpus examined consists of 202 syntactic clauses, 1433 words and 137 hesitations.

Hesitation analysis. Two types of hesitation were examined − unfilled pauses (UPs) and filled pauses (FPs). UPs were defined as periods of silence ≥ 200 milliseconds; these were identified and measured using an Ediswan pen oscillograph and pause detector. FPs consist of the following speech sounds: ah, er, um, etc. The mean duration of FPs was estimated to be approximately 300 milliseconds. The location of each hesitation was marked on the speech transcript. A distributional analysis of UPs and FPs with respect to syntactic clauses was carried out. The type of syntactic clause analysed was a surface structure clause (as opposed to a deep structure clause, see Chomsky 1965). Surface structure clauses longer than ten words were ignored as there were too few of them to allow reliable analysis. Hesitations occurring in the juncture between two clauses were classified as occupying the clause-initial position of the succeeding clause (see Boomer 1965, p. 84).

A visual analogue of the speech, identifying periods of pausing and phonation, was prepared in the manner described by Henderson *et al.* (1966). Thus each individual pause and period of phonation was plotted on a graph. Lines were fitted to represent changes in the pause/phonation ratio across time, in such a way as to minimize the deviation of local changes in these two variables from the lines (see Henderson *et al.* 1966, p. 208). This procedure was checked by two independent judges. Some minor adjustments were necessary before perfect agreement was reached. A transcript of the speech was made, and transition times between cycles and cycle phases were determined from the graphs and mapped into the transcripts, using the timer mixed on the video-screen to determine the precise temporal location of any given word in the speech corpus. Thus it was possible to determine which clauses constituted each cycle and each phase of the cycle.

Analysis of gaze. Subjects were filmed with Sony cameras, fitted with zoom lenses, and a split-screen video circuit was employed for the judgement of gaze (Technique B; see Chapter 2). The occurrence or non-occurrence of speaker gaze at the listener was noted at each word boundary in his speech. Gaze was judged from the video-screen. The inter-observer reliability for two independent judges in the scoring of gaze, that is, the percentage agreement between the two judges, was 94.6%.

RESULTS

Hesitation analysis

Temporal cycles. When individual pause and phonation periods were graphically represented, and lines fitted to represent changes in relative fluency across time, a cyclic pattern emerged, with hesitant phases (high pause/phonation ratio) alternating with fluent phases (low pause/phonation ratio): see Figure 3.1. In all, 20 complete cycles (both phases present) were observed, as well as seven incomplete cycles, bounded by speaker switches. The mean cycle time was found to be 21.88 seconds (SD = 15.68). 47.12% of all single hesitations (UPs or FPs), or combinations of UPs and FPs, occurred in the hesitant phases of these temporal cycles, compared with 52.88% in fluent phases.

The cycles contained a mean of 8.80 clauses, hesitant phases a mean of 3.57 clauses, and fluent phases a mean of 5.23 clauses. There was no significant difference in the length of clauses in hesitant and fluent phases (G = 0.220, $p > 0.05$; Sokal and Rohlf 1973).

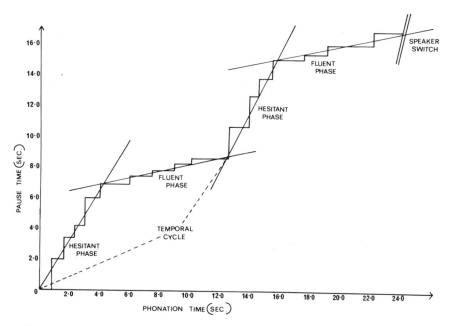

Figure 3.1 Sequential temporal patterns within one sample of spontaneous speech

Hesitations and syntactic clauses. The number and percentage of clauses occupied by a hesitation (UP or FP) was noted (see Table 3.2); 45.91% of all clauses contained a hesitation. Long clauses (6–10 words) were significantly more likely to contain a hesitation than short clauses (2–5 words) (G = 5.21, p < 0.05). This significant effect disappears, however, when the length of clauses, and number of possible positions for hesitations, is taken into consideration (G = 0.134, p < 0.05).

There was a significant tendency for UPs (G = 55.13, p < 0.001), FPs (G = 17.89, p < 0.001), and UPs or FPs (G = 79.23, p < 0.001) to occur in the clause-initial position. 54.02% of UPs, 57.69% of FPs, and 54.87% of hesitations (UPs or FPs) occurred at this point. There was also a significant tendency for hesitations to occur in the first half rather than the second half of clauses, even when hesitations at the clause-initial position are disregarded (G = 4.26, p < 0.05). 26.55% of hesitations occurred in the first half of clauses (excluding hesitations in the clause-initial position), compared with 15.04% in the second half. (3.54% of hesitations could not be classified in terms of their occurrence in the first or second half of clauses. These occurred in the middle of clauses containing an even number of words.) There was also a significant tendency for hesitations to occur in the clause-

Table 3.2 Number and percentage of clauses containing hesitations, whose mean length is also indicated

	Number containing hesitation(s)	Percentage containing hesitation(s)	Number containing hesitation in clause-initial position	Percentage containing hesitation in clause-initial position	Number of hesitations in clause-initial position	Mean length of hesitation in clause-initial position (milliseconds)
All clauses (2–10 words)	73	45.91	51	32.08	62	807
Short clauses (2–5 words)	38	38.38	28	28.28	32	676
Long clauses (6–10 words)	35	58.33	23	38.33	30	966

initial position of long clauses rather than short clauses (G = 4.168, $p < 0.05$). The mean length of hesitations preceding long clauses was also greater than the mean length of hesitations preceding short clauses (966 and 676 milliseconds respectively).

This evidence indicates that hesitations do cluster towards the beginnings of syntactic clauses, and this could be taken to suggest that the main encoding unit is the syntactic clause. However, if planning in speech does not transcend clause boundaries, then clauses executed without a hesitation must be examples of 'old well-organized speech' (Jackson 1878; Goldman-Eisler 1968). In a speech corpus like the one studied, 'automatic' speech is rare and thus, if the syntactic clause is the main unit of encoding, the majority of clauses should contain a hesitation (particularly at the clause-initial position). Table 3.2, however, reveals that only 32.08% of clauses had a hesitation in the clause-initial position.

It was also discovered that only 60.0% of the longest clauses studied (ten-word clauses), and 33.33% of eight-word clauses contained a hesitation in the clause-initial position. Furthermore, only 25.81% of three-word clauses and 35.29% of two-word clauses had a hesitation at any point in the clause.

Hesitations, syntactic clauses, and temporal cycles. The number and percentage of clauses, which fell differentially within hesitant or fluent phases of temporal cycles, and which contained a hesitation, were noted (see Table 3.3).

As expected, a higher proportion of clauses in hesitant phases of cycles contained hesitations than did clauses in fluent phases (53.03% and 41.30% respectively). In the case of clauses in hesitant phases of cycles, long clauses were significantly more likely to contain a hesitation than short clauses (G = 7.836, $p < 0.05$), but this was not significant for clauses in fluent phases of cycles (G = 0.918, $p > 0.05$).

There was a significant tendency for hesitations to occur in the clause-initial position in both the hesitant (G = 49.324, $p < 0.001$) and fluent phases of cycles (G = 31.300, $p < 0.001$). 60% of hesitations in hesitant phases of cycles occurred at the clause-initial position, compared with 50% of hesitations in fluent phases.

Hesitations were significantly more likely to occur in the clause-initial position of long clauses than short clauses, only in the case of clauses in hesitant phases of cycles (G = 4.682, $p < 0.05$). For clauses in fluent phases, G = 1.772 ($p > 0.05$).

The mean length of hesitations in the clause-initial position was also computed (see Table 3.3). The longest of these hesitations (mean 1205

Table 3.3 Number and percentage of clauses, within hesitant or fluent phases of temporal cycles, containing hesitations, whose mean length is indicated

	Hesitant phase of temporal cycle				
	Number containing hesitation(s)	*Percentage containing hesitation(s)*	*Number with hesitation at clause-initial position*	*Percentage with hesitation at clause-initial position*	*Mean length of hesitation (milliseconds)*
All clauses (2–10 words)	35	53.03	26	38.81	1053
Short clauses (2–5 words)	18	41.86	13	29.55	669
Long clauses (6–10 words)	17	73.91	13	56.52	1205
	Fluent phase of temporal cycle				
All clauses (2–10 words)	38	41.30	25	27.17	672
Short clauses (2–5 words)	20	36.36	15	27.27	682
Long clauses (6–10 words)	18	48.65	10	27.03	657

milliseconds) were those preceding long clauses in hesitant phases of cycles. There was no significant difference in the duration of hesitations in the clause-initial position of long and short clauses in fluent phases of cycles (mean durations 657 and 682 milliseconds, respectively).

Analysis of speaker gaze. Table 3.4 shows the probability of speaker gaze and gaze aversion at hesitations and fluent word transitions.

As predicted from a cognitive hypothesis of nonjuncture hesitations (i.e. hesitations not in the clause-initial position), gaze aversion was significantly more probable at such points than at fluent transitions ($G = 5.596$, $p < 0.05$). 50.94% of all such hesitations were accompanied by gaze aversion, compared with 34.01% of fluent transitions.

However, the probability of gaze aversion occurring at hesitations in the clause-initial position and at fluent transitions was not significantly different (G = 3.446, $p > 0.05$). 47.05% of hesitations in the clause-initial position were accompanied by gaze aversion. If this class of hesitations is decomposed into those which occurred in hesitant phases of temporal cycles and those which occurred in fluent phases, it becomes apparent that these two categories of hesitation behaved differently. Gaze aversion was significantly more probable during hesitations in the clause-initial position in hesitant phases, than at fluent transitions (G = 3.950, $p < 0.05$), but this was not significant in the case of similarly-located hesitations in fluent phases (G = 0.021, $p > 0.05$). The percentage of hesitations in the clause-initial position (in hesitant phases of cycles) accompanied by gaze aversion was found to be higher than the percentage of hesitations in other positions accompanied by gaze aversion (53.85% and 50.94%, respectively).

DISCUSSION

This study found that the distribution of hesitations in speech is affected both by syntactic units as well as by units considerably larger than individual syntactic clauses. It is interesting to note that the cycles identified in the present study were somewhat longer and more variable than the cycles described by Butterworth (1975). The mean cycle time in the present study was found to be 21.88 seconds (SD = 15.68), compared with 18 seconds (SD = 5.29) in the Butterworth study. These differences may be attributable to variations in the speech content in the two studies. The greater variability of cycles in the present study may be due to the fact that there was some

Table 3.4 Number of hesitations and fluent word transitions, accompanied by gaze or gaze aversion

Type of word transition	Gaze		Gaze aversion	
Hesitation, clause-initial position (hesitant phase)	12 ⎫		14 ⎫	
Hesitation, clause-initial position (fluent phase)	15 ⎭ 27		10 ⎭ 24	
Other hesitations (hesitant phase)	8 ⎫		15 ⎫	
Other hesitations (fluent phase)	18 ⎭ 26		12 ⎭ 27	
Fluent transitions	877		452	

standardization of speech content in the Butterworth study (subjects argued for or against a series of standard propositions).

Hesitations and syntactic clauses. The distribution of hesitations was found to be related to the syntactic structure of speech. There was a significant tendency for hesitations to occur towards the beginnings of clauses, especially in the clause-initial position (see Table 3.2). However, the apparent functional relationship between hesitations and clause planning was only observed in clauses in the hesitant phases of temporal cycles. In these phases it was observed that long clauses were significantly more likely to contain a hesitation than short clauses, especially in the clause-initial position. Moreover, the mean duration of hesitations in the clause-initial position of long clauses in hesitant phases, was almost double the mean duration of such hesitations in short clauses (1205 and 669 milliseconds, respectively, see Table 3.3). In the case of clauses in fluent phases, there was no significant difference in the relative probability of hesitations occurring in long and short clauses, and little difference in the mean duration of hesitations in the clause-initial position of these clauses (657 and 682 milliseconds). These results suggest that hesitations in the clause-initial position in hesitant phases of cycles may have a proximal, i.e. short-term, clause-planning function, in addition to a distal semantic planning function (Goldman-Eisler, 1967; Butterworth, 1975), whereas those hesitations in the clause-initial position in fluent phases of cycles seem to perform neither function. These conclusions are supported by the analysis of speaker gaze (see Table 3.4), which revealed that gaze aversion is significantly more probable at hesitations in the clause-initial position in hesitant phases of cycles, than at fluent transitions, but this was not found to be significant in the case of clauses in fluent phases. This analysis suggests that hesitations in the clause-initial position in hesitant phases of cycles do perform some cognitive function(s), and that similarly positioned hesitations in fluent phases probably do not. It may be hypothesized that the function of this latter set of hesitations is primarily social – in the case of UPs, to segment the speech and allow time for decoding by the listener (Reich 1975), and in the case of FPs to prevent listener interruption (Beattie 1977).

Hesitations, syntactic clauses and lexical predictability. One question which must be raised is whether the significant relationship observed between hesitations and syntactic clauses could be an artefact of the tendency of unpredictable lexical items to occur towards the beginnings of clauses (and especially in the first position in the clause). Boomer (1965) explicitly dismissed this possibility with the argument that 'primary stress typically occurs towards the end of a phonemic clause; almost invariably the last or next to last word in the clause receives the stress. And, as Berry (1953, p. 88) has shown, primary stress is negatively related to word frequency . . . Thus the high-information lexical words tend to occur towards the end of phonemic clauses'. A pilot study of the relationship between lexical unpredictability and clause position was performed on a sample of 30 clauses (15 hesitant phases of cycles, 15 from fluent phases). (The sample was randomly selected from the Butterworth (1972) corpus. Clauses varied in length from 3 to 14 words, and there were 191 words in the sample.) Transitional probability was measured using the Cloze procedure (Taylor 1953) which consists of deleting words from a text, and employing a number of judges to guess the deleted item. The fewer judges who guess correctly, the more unpredictable the item is held to be. In this application of the procedure, five protocols of each text were prepared, each with every fifth word deleted (each protocol has a different set of words deleted). Each of the five protocols was given to a set of five judges. Thus, each word in the text became associated with a Cloze score of 0, 1, 2, 3, 4, or 5, according to how many judges guessed it correctly.

Table 3.5 shows the relationship between mean Cloze score and clause position. It was discovered that there were significantly more high Cloze score items (4, 5), as opposed to low Cloze score items (0, 1), at the first position in the clause than elsewhere (G = 4.166, $p < 0.05$). (In the case of clauses beginning with either an indefinite or definite article, if the Cloze score of the following adjective or noun is considered rather than the Cloze score of the article itself, this is found to have no effect on the result.) 81.48% of clause-initial words were found to be high Cloze score items, compared with 59.02% of all other words in the corpus. There were also significantly more high Cloze score items in the first half than in the second half of clauses, even when clause-initial words are disregarded (G = 5.748,

Table 3.5 Relationship between mean Cloze score and position of word in clauses in hesitant and fluent phases of temporal cycles

Phase of temporal cycle	Clause-initial word	First half of clause	Second half of clause	Mean
Hesitant	4.13	3.16	2.47	3.07
Fluent	3.27	3.31	2.31	2.87

$p < 0.05$). 69.45% of words from the first half of clauses were high Cloze score items compared with 45.45% from the second half of clauses. These results are even more striking when it is recalled that measures of transitional probability, such as Cloze score, are sensitive to the effects of contextual accumulation (Aborn *et al.* 1959; Burke and Schiavetti 1975), and thus, *ceteris paribus*, words occurring later in a clause should be more predictable than words occurring earlier in a clause.

These results thus suggest that the tendency of hesitations to occur towards the beginnings of clauses is not an artefact of lexical unpredictability, since there is a tendency for the more unpredictable words to occur towards the end of clauses.

Conclusions

PATTERNS OF HESITATION IN SPONTANEOUS SPEECH

Despite the fact that hesitations were found to cluster towards the beginning of syntactic clauses (and the subsequent demonstration that this was not an artefact of lexical unpredictability), the hypothesis that the clause is the fundamental unit of encoding (Boomer 1965; Fodor *et al.* 1974) did not receive support in this study. Three lines of evidence ran counter to this hypothesis. The first is the observation that the majority of clauses did not contain a hesitation in the clause-initial position, or at any location in the clause. 81.25% of four-word clauses did not contain a hesitation in the clause-initial position and 74.19% of three-word clauses were completely fluent. If it is accepted that hesitations are necessary for cognitive planning in speech (see Beattie and Bradbury 1979), then either it must be assumed that the majority of utterances in the present corpus did not require planning and were therefore 'old, well-organized and automatic' (Jackson 1878), or it must be accepted that planning in speech typically transcends clause boundaries. According to the latter hypothesis, fluent clauses are not 'automatic' verbalizations, but new utterances resulting from planning in a preceding part of the utterance. This hypothesis is supported by study of the speech transcripts which reveals little in the way of 'automatic' speech. The second line of evidence is the emergence of a macrostructure in the hesitations data which suggests that higher-order units (in the region of 8.80 clauses) are involved in the planning of speech. The third line of evidence derives from two sources – firstly from analysis of the relationship between clause length and the probability (and duration) of hesitations, and secondly from analysis of speaker gaze. Both analyses suggest that the functional relationship between hesitations and the planning of clauses is context-specific, holding only for clauses in the hesitant phases of temporal cycles. These observations suggest that the hypothesis that planning in speech universally proceeds on a clause-by-clause basis is incorrect.

The evidence obtained in the present study is consonant with the hypothesis that the main encoding units are suprasentential in scope and therefore probably semantic in nature (Butterworth 1975, 1976). However, execution of the initial parts of these units does typically commence before the semantic planning of the entire unit is complete. A mean of 3.57 clauses were executed during the hesitant phases. Moreover, it is interesting to note that this speech seems no more predictable, in terms of Cloze score, than speech in fluent phases (there were 50 high and 25 low Cloze score items in hesitant phases, compared with 44 high and 25 low Cloze score items in fluent phases, $G = 0.450$, $p > 0.05$; see also Table 3.5), and it does appear to be planned on a clause-by-clause basis. This evidence thus suggests that both semantic and syntactic encoding units are implicated in the generation of spontaneous speech, with the latter type less extensive than the former. A social hypothesis can perhaps account for the fact that speech does occur in these planning phases; namely that, if output were suspended until a complete semantic plan was formulated, then considerably longer (but fewer) hesitations would be necessary for the generation of speech. One consequence of this would be that listener's attempts to gain control of the conversation would become more frequent and probably more successful (Beattie 1977). By speaking during semantic planning phases, the speaker can redistribute planning time (using more frequent, but shorter, hesitations) whilst keeping the listener interested, and lessening the probability of interruption. This hypothesis does receive some support from a study by Beattie and Bradbury (1979) which demonstrated that subjects can, when necessary, modify their temporal planning structure in mono-logue, without significantly affecting speech content. It also, of course, predicts that the structure of temporal cycles will be sensitive to the social situation. In other words, that social context will greatly affect basic language production patterns.

The Organization of a Speaker's Nonverbal Behaviour in Conversation

Our nature consists in motion; complete rest is death.

PASCAL
Pensées (1670)

Introduction

This chapter explores the organization of two central components of nonverbal behaviour in conversation. The two components under investigation are speaker eye-gaze and speaker hand movement and gesture.

Gaze – that is, looking at another person – is of central importance in social behaviour. We both send signals with our eyes and receive them. As Erving Goffman said in an interview in the *New York Times* (12 February 1969), 'Eyes, you know, are the great intruders'. They intrude into every aspect of social interaction. Michael Argyle and Mark Cook (1976), in their book *Gaze and Mutual Gaze*, outlined how gaze and speech are connected. The following list is included here to highlight the number of different functions of gaze in interaction. However, a number of the specific functions suggested by Argyle and Cook will be challenged or qualified later in this book.

Argyle and Cook say:

Gaze is intricately connected with language, in the following ways:

1 *As a visible signal*

(a) Long glances are used by speaker as full-stop signals, and for other grammatical breaks.

(b) Glances are used by speakers to emphasise particular words or phrases, or to make the whole utterance more persuasive. Other kinds of commentary on the utterance can be given by varying facial expression.

(c) The line of regard is used to point at persons or things, e.g. to suggest who should speak next.

(d) Glances are used by listeners to indicate continued attention and willingness to listen. Aversion of gaze means lack of interest or disapproval.

(e) Glances made by listeners after particular points of an utterance act as reinforcers, and encourage the speaker to produce more of the same.

(f) Glances made by listeners vary in meaning with facial expression, including that in the region of the eyes; raised eyebrows indicate surprise, fully raised eyebrows disbelief; lowered eyebrows puzzlement, fully lowered eyebrows anger.

(g) Gaze is one signal among others for the communication of interpersonal attitudes; however, there is no linkage with speech here, glances are simply longer or shorter and accompanied by different facial expression.

2 *As a channel*

(a) Speakers look up at grammatical pauses to obtain feedback on how utterances are being received, and to see if others are willing for them to carry on speaking.

(b) Listeners look at speakers a lot of the time, in order to study their facial expressions, and their direction of gaze.

3 *Aversion of gaze*

Gaze is used intermittently, so that when it is used it gives a signal. The reason that people do not look all the time is probably to avoid overload of information (p. 121).

Patterns of speaker eye-gaze

A number of these functions depend critically upon the linguistic context in which gaze, especially speaker gaze, occurs. A detailed description of the interconnections between gaze and speech in conversation would thus be of the highest priority. The majority of studies on speaker gaze in conversation have however tended to confine themselves to attempting to measure the amount rather than the precise patterning of this form of behaviour. The studies which have explored the patterning of gaze with speech have often employed rather ubiquitous and sometimes vague categories of language such as 'remark' or 'question'. As a result, the patternings of gaze which have been reported have shown considerable variation. Libby (1970), for example, observed that in an interview in which the interviewer gazed steadily at subjects who were replying to questions, nearly 85% broke gaze during their reply, although less than 10% broke gaze before the end of the question. Here, 'embarrassing' and 'unembarrassing', 'personal' and 'impersonal' questions, demanding long and short answers, were combined in the analysis of gaze patterning. Nielsen (1962) observed that subjects broke gaze at the beginning of a 'remark' in conversation in almost 45% of all cases, and they looked at their interviewer at the end of a 'remark' in about 50% of all cases. But in these studies we end up with various gross averages. The nature of the 'remarks' presumably varied and presumably also affected subjects' gaze, but this was not really analysed.

The most intensive analysis of the patterning of gaze in conversation, and the only study to focus on possible planning units within speech, was the study by Adam Kendon (1967). One of his principal observations was that speakers tended to look at listeners more during fluent speech than during hesitant speech (50% of the time spent speaking fluently as compared to only 20% of the time speaking hesitantly). Kendon hypothesized that speaker gaze frequently performs a monitoring function (as we discussed earlier) and that such monitoring may interfere with the planning of spontaneous speech. Speakers may therefore avert gaze during the hesitant periods in spontaneous speech.

Kendon also described the patterning of gaze with respect to 'phrases' and 'phrase boundary pauses' (some of the principal units of analysis in his corpus), and found that the speaker tended to look at the listener as he approached the end of a phrase and continued to look during the phrase boundary pause, but averted his gaze as the next phrase began. It was also observed that 'utterances' terminated with prolonged gaze (one problem with this study, however, as I have already pointed out was that the linguistic units around which the analyses were based – 'phrase', 'utterance', etc. – were not defined. Indeed, some linguistic units had to wait eleven years before an explicit definition was provided; see Kendon 1978). Kendon hypothesized that gaze had a signalling function at the ends of utterances, specifically concerned with the transmission of information to the listener about the appropriateness of a response at these points.

The aim of the following study is to analyse the distribution of gaze with respect to temporal cycles (of the kind which emerged in Chapter 3). The experimental evidence presented in that chapter suggests that cognitive processing is asymmetrically distributed throughout the cycles. More cognitive planning seems to occur in the hesitant phase of the cycle than in the fluent phase, since both short-term clausal planning and more long-term semantic planning occur in the hesitant phase, whereas the evidence suggests that only immediate lexical decisions are made in the fluent phase (Butterworth and Beattie 1978). Thus, if we assume that speaker gaze has a monitoring function, then we would predict an approximately inverse relationship between the relative hesitancy of speech and the amount of speaker gaze at the listener.

Previous research has also suggested that these cycles represent semantic units in speech; cycles correspond to 'ideas' in the speech text (Butterworth 1975). Thus, these cycles will probably function as important units in conversation and speakers may seek to avoid any interruption of ideas by inhibiting (where possible) cues such as eye-gaze which might elicit listener responses during the cycles, and by employing such cues more forcefully and more frequently at the boundaries of the units. Thus, it can be predicted that speaker eye-gaze at the boundaries of these units will be very common in conversation. The method of microanalysis is identical to that employed in Chapter 3 (except that clauses up to 12 words long were considered). Frame-by-frame analysis of video-recordings of dyadic tutorials (recorded at Cambridge University) was again carried out and the relationship between spontaneous speech and speaker eye-gaze studied in detail.

RESULTS

Gaze and mean hesitancy of phase

The number of hesitant and fluent phases in the temporal cycles dominated by gaze or gaze aversion (i.e. with more than or less than 50% gaze, respectively) were noted, as was the slope of each phase measured in degrees; a 45° slope indicates an equal proportion of pausing and phonation, a 0° slope indicates uninterrupted phonation, a 90° slope indicates extended pausing. The number of changes in gaze state per phase, and the number of words separating each change of gaze state were also recorded (see Table 4.1).

A difference in the relative number of hesitant and fluent phases dominated by gaze did emerge, but this difference failed to reach significance ($G = 2.512$, $p < 0.2$). There was a tendency for both types of phase to be accompanied by more gaze than gaze aversion,

Table 4.1 Patterns of gaze in temporal cycles

Phase type	Phase dominated by gaze or gaze aversion	No. of H and F phases dominated by gaze or gaze aversion	Mean slope of each phase (in degrees)	Mean no. of changes in gaze state per phase	Mean no. of words separating each change in gaze states
Hesitant	Gaze	13	47.07	2.39	10.04
	Gaze aversion	9	47.55	1.67	11.51
Fluent	Gaze	20	6.30	2.60	12.65
	Gaze aversion	4	13.77	4.25	12.41

indicating a high level of speaker gaze generally in this type of situation; however, in the case of fluent phases the trend was much more pronounced. The slopes (reflecting the mean percentage of hesitation per phase) of the various hesitant and fluent phases were then compared. In the case of fluent phases, those phases dominated by gaze aversion tended to be significantly more hesitant than the phases dominated by gaze (mean slopes 13.77° and 6.30° respectively, Mann–Whitney U test, U = 12, $p < 0.05$, two-tailed test). In the case of hesitant phases there was no significant difference in the slopes of those phases dominated by gaze or gaze aversion (mean slopes 47.07° and 47.55° respectively, Mann–Whitney U test, U = 38.5, $p > 0.05$, two-tailed).

It should be noted that the dominance of a phase by gaze or gaze aversion is not simply attributable to there being more phonation or hesitation in the phase, since 6 of the 13 hesitant phases dominated by gaze had slopes which were greater than 45° (i.e. there was more pausing than phonation), and none of the fluent phases had slopes greater than 45°, although four of these phases were dominated by gaze aversion. In a number of cases, the distribution of gaze can be clearly seen not to be optimal for cognitive purposes. For example, two hesitant phases had slopes of 90°, i.e. they consisted of prolonged pausing, but these were accompanied by uninterrupted gaze, and not gaze aversion.

Table 4.1 also seems to reveal differences in the stability of gaze in hesitant and fluent phases dominated by gaze or gaze aversion, but such differences largely disappear when the number of words is taken into consideration (last column). There was an overall mean of 2.5 changes in gaze state per phase, which suggests that there was a change approximately every 1.76 clauses. There was a non-clausal hesitation every 12.9 words, and a hesitation approximately every eight words, which would suggest that gaze behaviour is more stable than it should be, if it were simply reflecting each fluent–hesitant–fluent transition. There should be $2n$ changes in gaze state for every n hesitations, and thus we would predict a mean of approximately six words to separate each gaze state, if gaze were simply reflecting the location of individual hesitations.

Gaze and syntactic clauses. Gaze across the first 12 boundary locations of clauses between 2 and 12 words in length was analysed, and the percentage of each boundary location occupied by gaze was calculated (see Table 4.2).

The randomness of these percentages was tested using a one-sample runs test. When all clauses were considered, the distribution of gaze

Table 4.2 Percentage of boundary locations in syntactic clauses accompanied by gaze

Phase Type	Boundary Location											
	1	2	3	4	5	6	7	8	9	10	11	12
Hesitant	60.27	50.68	56.76	57.14	57.14	58.33	55.17	57.14	68.75	71.42	80.00	50.00
Fluent	60.61	64.65	59.79	65.85	66.15	69.09	72.73	72.73	75.00	70.00	76.92	85.71
Both	60.47	58.72	58.15	63.55	64.83	68.49	62.96	66.00	73.53	70.70	77.50	75.00

was found to be random ($r = 4$); similarly with clauses falling within hesitant phases ($r = 9$). However, in the case of clauses in fluent phases, the distribution was not random ($r = 2$, $p < 0.05$). The percentage of successive boundary locations occupied by gaze tended to increase in a non-random fashion. The mean percentage increase from boundary location 1 to boundary location 12 was 25.10%, in the case of syntactic clauses, within fluent phases. It should also be noted that clauses in fluent phases tended to have significantly more overall gaze than syntactic clauses in hesitant phases, when the percentage of gaze at each boundary location was compared (Wilcoxon matched pairs signed-ranks test, two-tail, $T = 6$, $p < 0.01$).

The second analysis sought to determine if syntactic clauses tended to terminate with gaze. This time, the number of instances of gaze at the first and last position of clauses between 2 and 12 words in length were compared. This was carried out separately for clauses in the hesitant and fluent phases of the cycles. In neither case did a significant effect emerge: not in the case of clauses in hesitant phases (Wilcoxon test, $T = 16.5$, $p > 0.05$), nor in the case of clauses in fluent phases (Wilcoxon test, $T = 15$, $p > 0.05$). The mean percentage of gaze at clause junctures was found to be 60.47%.

The significant results in the first analysis but not in the second indicate that clause length is an important factor. The longer the clause, the more likely it is to terminate with gaze. This is especially the case with clauses in the fluent phases of cycles.

Gaze, temporal cycles and clause junctures. The incidence of gaze at clause junctures nearest the terminal points of temporal cycles was compared with the incidence of gaze at all other clause junctures (see Table 4.3).

Gaze was found to occur significantly more frequently at clause junctures nearest the terminal points of temporal cycles than at other clause junctures ($G = 3.836$, $p < 0.05$). The mean percentage gaze at clause junctures nearest the terminal points of temporal cycles was 81.82%.

The gaze which coincided with the ends of temporal cycles was not a discrete cueing signal. This terminal gaze was initiated a mean of 1.83 syntactic clauses before the end of a cycle (a mean of 12.0 words earlier), and it continued into the subsequent cycle for a mean of 1.44 clauses (mean of 5.7 words). These figures suggest that such gaze does not function solely as a signal that an appropriate listener response point has been reached. They suggest instead that such gaze performs a dual function – firstly, that of signalling, and conversational regulation, and secondly that of monitoring the reception of the semantic unit by the listener.

Filled hesitation and temporal cycles. The patterning of gaze and proportion of gaze within individual hesitant and fluent phases is not simply a function of a basic cognitive variable plus a compatible reciprocal social signalling function. There is considerable divergence from the patterns which would be optimal on cognitive grounds. An analysis was performed to determine if this divergence had any significant effects on the speech produced. The amount of filled hesitation (consisting of FPs, repetitions, false starts, and parenthetic remarks occurring in each cycle was analysed. The measure should prove sensitive to deficits in forward planning (see Chapter 3). G_0, G_1 type cycles ($n = 7$) are cycles in which hesitant phases are dominated by gaze aversion and fluent phases by gaze. G_1, G_1 type cycles ($n = 11$) are those in which both phases are dominated by gaze (there were only two instances of G_1, G_0 type cycles, and no examples of a G_0, G_0 type cycle, in the present corpus). Thus, if speaker gaze during semantic planning phases does interfere with cognitive processing, there should be more filled hesitation in both phases of G_1, G_1 cycles than in G_0, G_1 cycles. Table 4.4 reveals that the false start variable was in fact sensitive to the mismatch between gaze behaviour and cognitive processing.

There were significantly more false starts in the G_1, G_1 cycles than in G_0, G_1 cycles (Mann–Whitney U test, $U = 15$, $p < 0.05$, two-

Table 4.3 Incidence of gaze at clause junctures nearest termination of temporal cycle compared with the incidence at all other clause junctures.

	Gaze	Gaze aversion
Clause junctures nearest termination of cycle	18	4
Other clause junctures	100	71

Talk

Table 4.4 Filled hesitation and temporal cycles

		Type of cycle					
	Hesitation type	G_0, G_1 ($n = 7$)			G_1, G_1 ($n = 11$)		
		H	F	Both	H	F	Both
Mean	False starts	1.28	0	1.28	3.64	1.45	5.09
Hesitation rate (in words)	Parenthetic remarks	0.86	1.43	2.29	0.73	1.27	2.00
	Repetition	0.14	0.57	0.71	0.27	0.37	0.64
	Filled pauses	0.86	1.28	2.14	0.55	0.73	1.28
Mean	False starts	0.0689	0	0.0221	0.1558	0.0609	0.1079
Hesitation rate, per unit word spoken	Parenthetic remarks	0.0463	0.0364	0.0396	0.0312	0.0535	0.0424
	Repetition	0.0075	0.0145	0.0123	0.0116	0.0155	0.0136
	Filled pauses	0.0463	0.0326	0.0370	0.0235	0.0306	0.0271

tailed). False starts were approximately five times as common, per unit word spoken, in G_1, G_1 cycles than G_0, G_1 cycles. There was also an increase in rate of repetition and parenthetic remarks, per unit word, in G_1, G_1 cycles, although these differences failed to reach significance.

DISCUSSION

One significant feature of the results obtained in this study was the high proportion of gaze whilst speaking. The mean percentage was 66.8%. (All speakers analysed were male in the present study, and only one of the interactions involved a mixed-sex pair). The comparable figures from Argyle and Ingham (1972) for the percentage of gaze whilst talking was 31% for same sex (male) pairs, and 52% for mixed-sex pairs, with the man talking. Furthermore, Exline and Winters' (1965) observation that amount of gaze in conversation is inversely related to the cognitive difficulty of the topic of conversation, would lead one to predict a lower overall level of gaze in the present study, compared with other studies, since the topic under discussion in the present study was certainly more difficult than the conversational topics in many of the studies of gaze and speech. Cambridge supervisions and seminars do after all usually involve complex topics. However, a number of social considerations can be used to account for the high rate. Firstly, in the present study subjects were acquainted, whereas in most previous studies they were unacquainted. The level of gaze between intimates tends to be higher than between strangers (Argyle and Dean 1965). Furthermore, the distance between the interactants was fixed, in the present study, at a distance which might perhaps have exceeded the distance that acquaintances would normally choose (some subjects spontaneously commented on this). Thus the intimacy equilibrium model of Argyle and Dean (1965), would suggest that the high rate of gaze whilst talking was to compensate for the increased distance. A compensatory relationship between proximity and gaze, given a certain level of intimacy, has found considerable empirical support (Argyle and Ingham 1972; Knight, Langmeter and Landgren 1973; Schulze and Barefoot 1974; Stephenson, Rutter and Dore 1973; Patterson 1973). It may also be hypothesized that the high degree of listener attentiveness produced by supervision-type situations contributed to the high gaze rate, since Cook and Smith (1972) (cited by Argyle and Cook 1976), found that the amount of gaze whilst speaking increases when a confederate looks continuously. Thus the high rate of gaze observed would seem to be consistent with a number of other observations.

The analysis of the relationship between the temporal cycles of speech and the macropatterns of gaze revealed a loosely coordinated system. The patterning of gaze did seem to reflect the gross temporal structure of the speech. These results appear to conflict with other studies which have found that a Markov chain structure, with a 300 millisecond transition state, can account for the distribution of pausing and phonation in speech (Jaffe and Feldstein 1970), and a first-order Markov chain structure with a 600 millisecond transition state, can account for the dyadic gaze states occurring in conversation (Natale 1976). (These studies had suggested that the onset of pausing or eye-gaze in conversation was almost entirely predictable from the preceding interval – in one case 300 milliseconds, and in the other 600 milliseconds.) It should be added that such studies ignore the functional interdependence of speech and gaze by attempting to describe the pattern of two obviously related phenomena in isolation. It remains to be seen to what extent the Markov description of pause/phonation occurrences and of the gaze accompanying speech is compatible with the observations made in this study. It may be possible to reconcile the two sets of observations. For example, it can be suggested that the Markov structure of pausing and phonation in speech, reported by Jaffe and Feldstein (1970), may have resulted from gross averaging of samples of speech of different complexity, some of which may not have been sufficiently complex to involve a temporal rhythm (see Goldman-Eisler 1968). The Natale (1976) study may have involved speech which did not display a temporal rhythm, given the rather simple topic of conversation (subjects were asked to have a conversation on their impressions of life at university). Alternatively, analyses which have shown that a first-order, as opposed to an nth-order, Markov process best accounts for the pattern of dyadic gaze, may even be compatible with the results of the present study, by accounting for the local variation of gaze within the macropatterns observed. One point should be remembered about these macropatterns, namely that variation in the overall length of the cycles was very large (the mean was 21.88 seconds and the standard deviation was 15.68). Thus it cannot presently be contended that a higher-order Markov structure of any identifiable order would be a better fit for the data, given the enormous degree of temporal uncertainty in the overall length of the cycles. Only careful research in the future will determine which mathematical model best fits the patterning of gaze accompanying complex speech which itself displays a rhythmic structure.

The patterning of gaze and proportion of gaze within individual hesitant and fluent phases was shown not to be simply a function of a basic cognitive variable, plus a compatible, reciprocal social signalling function. One possible source of this divergence is the social pressure on interactants in conversations to attempt to create a favourable impression. Research has indicated that various gaze patterns are differently evaluated, e.g. Argyle *et al.* (1974) found that subjects disliked people who stared continuously. Exline and Eldridge (1967) found that subjects thought that speakers were more likely to mean what they said if they looked at them. Kleck and Nuessle (1968) found that confederates who looked only a small proportion of the time were described as 'defensive' or 'evasive', whereas those who looked a lot (80% of the time) were described as 'friendly', 'mature' or 'sincere'. Cook and Smith (1975) found that there was a tendency for confederates who averted gaze to be seen as nervous and lacking in confidence. In fact, positive evaluation was positively correlated with the amount of gaze. Furthermore, Kendon and Cook (1969) found that subjects preferred individuals who gave long glances, and evaluated less favourably those who gazed frequently and with shorter glances. The tendency for gaze to be more stable than predicted, on cognitive grounds, in the present study, may be attributable to the fact that subjects were attempting to create a favourable impression by using relatively long glances rather than more rapid short glances. The high proportion of gaze accompanying certain hesitant periods may also be due to the same basic effect. Total gaze aversion would have been the cognitively optimal strategy in a number of cases, at least in terms of the planning of speech, but total gaze aversion is disliked by subjects (Argyle *et al.* 1974), perhaps for obvious reasons! The fact that social factors may interfere with the cognitively-optimal pattern-ing of gaze, and that this may result in decrements in verbal performance, would indicate that it may be fruitful to look closely at certain delineable populations who show marked abnormalities in both gaze behaviour and speech. Differences from the norm in apparently separate aspects of behaviour may be accountable for in terms of an abnormality in a basic organizational principle.

CONCLUSION

This study demonstrated that speaker eye-gaze is connected in an intricate pattern with the flow of spontaneous speech. Speakers tend to look most at listeners during the most fluent phases of speech. If they fail to avert their eyes during the planning periods in spontaneous speech, there is a marked increase in speech disturbances. The temporal cycles which seem to reflect some of the basic planning processes of spontaneous speech have a great influence on the patterning of speaker eye-gaze. But some divergence from what might be expected on purely cognitive grounds was observed. It was suggested that this was probably to do with social processes. Speakers have to plan what they are going to say, but, in addition, they often wish to make a good impression – 'competent', 'believable', 'knowledgeable', etc. – by looking directly at the listener. This unfortunately can sometimes lead to problems where the frequency of various types of error in speech increases dramatically. Conversations are clearly sometimes difficult to handle.

Speaker movement and gesture

An obvious characteristic of conversation is that speakers (and listeners) seldom remain perfectly still during it. In the case of speakers hand gestures appear particularly common. There appear to be two fundamentally different kinds of speaker hand activity: one class of movement, which is not speech-related, involves self-stimulation (e.g. finger-rubbing, scratching, etc.). These have been termed body-focussed movements (Freedman and Hoffman 1967). The second class of movement is speech-related, and a subset of these movements does seem to reflect the meaning of what is said. These movements can be termed speech-focussed movements (SFMs).

There have been two principle theoretical orientations concerning the significance of speaker movement (it should be noted that most early studies did not differentiate speech-focussed and body-focussed movements). One view, based in the psychoanalytic tradition, has held that such movements can reveal a speaker's emotional or affective state (Freud 1905; Deutsch 1947, 1952; Feldman 1959). A second view has held that such movements constitute an alternative channel of communication, either augmenting the verbal component (Baxter *et al.* 1968) or substituting for it (Mahl *et al.* 1959), although no demonstrable benefit from these nonverbal 'signals' has been found to accrue to the listener, except in the case of the communication of shape information, in an experimental situation requiring subjects to describe two-dimensional drawings (Graham and Argyle 1975). However, Dobrogaev (cited by Schlauch 1936) found that the elimination of gesture resulted in marked changes in speech performance, with decreased fluency, impaired articulation, and a reduced vocabulary size. Graham and Heywood (1975) also found that the elimination of gesture (subjects were instructed to keep their arms folded) produced some changes in speech content (for example a significant increase in expressions denoting spatial relationships, and a significant reduction in the use of demonstratives), as well as a significant increase in the proportion of time spent pausing. Graham and Heywood concluded that this result suggested that gestures normally facilitate language production, at least on certain topics (i.e. those involving spatial descriptions).

There have been other attempts to relate various types of bodily movement to structural units of language. Birdwhistell (1970) described the relationship between 'kinesic markers' and various parts of speech (pronouns, verbs, etc.). Kendon (1972) concentrated on larger units of language, but unfortunately used an extremely small sample (1½ minutes from one speaker). His conclusion was that 'each speech unit is distinguished by a pattern of movement and of body-part involvement in movement. The larger the speech unit, the greater the difference in the form of movement, and the body parts involved.' Bull and Brown (1977), using a much larger sample, studied the relationship between posture change and speech, and found that significant changes in trunk and leg postures by the speaker only occurred while new pieces of information were being introduced into the conversation.

The only studies to attempt to relate movement to the psychological processes underlying speech have been by Dittmann (1972) and McNeill (1975). Dittmann (1972) investigated the relationship between an undifferentiated class of 'nervous' movements of the head, hands and feet and phonemic clauses. He discovered that these movements clustered towards the beginnings of hesitant phonemic clauses and thus concluded, following Boomer (1965), that these nervous movements were motor manifestations of the speech encoding process. McNeill (1975) presented a theory of the relationship between gesture and speech (this unfortunately preceded detailed naturalistic description of their interrelations). This theory was based on the assumption that speech is integrated in terms of the syntagma which is, according to Kozhevnikov and Chistovisch (1965 p. 74), 'one meaning unit, which is pronounced as a single output'. (Syntagmas have similar dimensions to phonemic clauses, but considerably more emphasis is laid on semantics in their definition.) McNeill argued that throughout development, speech remains directly adapted to the sensory-motor and representational levels of cognitive functioning but with time there occurs a 'semiotic extension' of the basic speech mechanism to cover more abstract levels of operational thought. Gestures, according to McNeill, have their origin in this semiotic extension, but they correspond to the sensory-motor schemas underlying speech. The evidence for the theory (based on observations of individuals simultaneously performing tasks, such as mental paper-folding, and describing their actions) revealed that iconic gestures were initiated with the onset of speech associated with the basic action schemas, and were prolonged for the duration of these schemas. This theory, however, can be challenged on a number of accounts. First, the assumption that the fundamental unit of encoding is of the same dimension as a clause can be questioned (see Chapter 3). Second, the relevance of such restricted data for natural movement and speech may be doubted.

The evidence purporting to the existence of higher-order units of language planning, described in Chapter 3, suggested that studies of the relationship between psychological processes in speech and nonverbal behaviour should consider units of language larger than individual phonemic clauses and syntagmas. This is the aim of the following study (reported in more detail in Butterworth and Beattie 1978). The sample of conversation again consisted of supervisions and a seminar.

PROCEDURE

The total duration of speech analysed was 849.8 seconds, chosen in a fairly random fashion. The only constraints on this selection were firstly that the speaker's turn in the conversation had to be at least 30 seconds, so that temporal cycles could be identified, and secondly that some speaker hand movements had to occur. Data were available from seven speakers.

The temporal analysis was carried out as follows: temporal cycles were identified in the manner described in Chapter 3, and thereby independently of the location of the gestures, since only sound could be detected by the signal detector. A timer (to one hundredth of a second) was mixed on to the video-recordings, so the precise timing of words and gestures could be achieved, and the result matched to temporal cycle data.

The present analysis concentrates on three classes of hand and arm movement.

(1) Speech-focussed movements (SFMs). All movements of the arm or hand except self-touching (e.g. finger-rubbing, scratching). This class includes gestures, 'batonic' movements and other simple movements.

(2) Gestures. More complex movements which appear to bear some semantic relation to the verbal component of the message.

(3) Changes in the basic equilibrium position of the arms and hands, that is, changes in the position where the hands return to after making an SFM.

The classification of each movement into one of the above categories was performed by two independent judges, and disagreements resolved by joint rechecking of the videotape. The exact time of the initiation of each SFM and equilibrium change could be obtained by utilizing the slow-motion facility of the VTR. The points were located on the pause/phonation plots, and on transcripts of the verbal output. In the case of gestures, the exact time between the initiation of the gesture and the first phoneme of the word with which it was associated was noted. The time of each equilibrium change was also noted.

RESULTS

The number of SFMs, gestures and SFMs minus gestures occurring per unit time during pauses or periods of phonation in planning and execution phases was analysed (see Table 4.5).

Table 4.5 The rate of production (per 1000 seconds) of SFMs, gestures and SFMs minus gestures during pauses and phonation in hesitant and fluent phases of temporal cycles

	Phase of cycle	*Pause*	*Phonation*	*Mean rate*
SFMs	Hesitant	118.4	191.9	153.0
	Fluent	341.0	199.7	226.2
	Mean rate	196.5	197.5	
Gestures	Hesitant	59.2	44.3	52.2
	Fluent	280.1	106.9	139.4
	Mean rate	136.7	89.6	
SFMs–gestures	Hesitant	59.2	147.6	100.9
	Fluent	60.9	92.8	86.8
	Mean rate	59.8	107.9	

The analysis revealed that SFMs occurred most frequently per unit time during fluent phases. The highest incidence of this class of behaviours was in pauses in the fluent phases. SFMs were approximately three times more frequent per unit time during such pauses than during pauses in the hesitant phases.

Gestures yielded an essentially similar distribution but in the case of gestures the trends were much more pronounced. Gestures were approximately five times as frequent per unit time during pauses in the fluent phases than during pauses in the hesitant phases. Gestures were also almost three times as frequent during pauses in the fluent phase as during periods of phonation in the fluent phase.

The residual class of SFMs minus gestures displayed a very different distribution. This time there was no overall difference in the number occurring per unit time during pauses in the hesitant and fluent phases and these behaviours were most common during periods of phonation, particularly in hesitant phases.

An ANOVA revealed that speech-focussed movements were significantly more frequent per unit time in the fluent phases of the cycle than in the hesitant phases ($F = 8.65$, d.f. $= 1$, $p < 0.05$). Furthermore there was a significant phase/activity interaction effect: in the hesitant phase, SFMs are more frequent during periods of phonation, whereas in the fluent phase SFMs are significantly more frequent during periods of hesitation ($F = 7.60$, d.f. $= 1$, $p < 0.05$).

When SFMs were split into gestures and non-gestural SFMs, an ANOVA revealed a significant interaction between movement type and specific location in the cycle. Non-gestural SFMs were most frequent per unit time in periods of phonation in the hesitant phase whereas gestures were most frequent per unit time during pauses in the fluent phases ($F = 3.15$, d.f. $= 3$, $p < 0.05$). Gestures were least frequent during periods of phonation in the hesitant phase.

This distributional difference between gestures and other SFMs suggests a functional difference. SFMs other than gestures consist mainly of simple batonic movements, and their close relation to periods of actual phonation in both hesitant and fluent phases indicates that a common-sense interpretation of them as emphasis markers is well-founded. The asymmetry in the distribution of gestures suggests, on the other hand, that these are not mere emphatic markers, but are functionally related to planning. Since they are relatively infrequent in the hesitant phase itself, they are not connected with the ideational planning process but with the lexical planning process. This hypothesis is supported by their close association with pauses in the fluent phase.

Further evidence of the functional distinction between gestures and SFMs is to be found by comparing their distributions in respect of the form-class of the words they are associated with (see Table 4.6). Gestures are heavily concentrated on nouns (41.3%), verbs (23.8%), and adjectives (15.9%) − classes which contain most of the unpredictable lexical items. Other SFMs, however, are much more evenly spaced over form-classes.

The initiation of gestures usually precedes, and never follows, the words they are associated with, the mean delay being around 800 milliseconds with a range of 100 milliseconds−2.50 seconds (Table 4.7). The length of delay seems unaffected by the position in that clause: again arguing for the connection of gestures with lexical selection, independent of any higher-level plans that determine the syntactic shape of the output.

The relationship between changes in the basic equilibrium position of the arm and hands, phasal transition points and clause junctures was analysed (see Table 4.8). A significant tendency for changes in the basic equilibrium position to correspond to both the terminal points of hesitant phases ($G = 22.118$, $p < 0.001$), and to the terminal points of fluent phases ($G = 39.336$, $p < 0.001$) was observed. Changes in equilibrium position were also found to coincide with junctures between clauses ($G = 61.448$, $p < 0.001$). These results provide further evidence that the hesitant and fluent phases, identified from changes in the gross temporal patterning of the speech, have some underlying psychological significance.

Table 4.6 Proportion of gestures (and SFMs minus gestures) associated with syntactic classes

	Noun	Verb	Adj.	Adv.	Pronoun	Prep.	Conj.	Dem. Adj.	Relative Pronoun	Inter- jections	Etcetera
Percent gestures	41.3	23.8	15.9	1.6	6.3	6.3	3.2	1.6			
Percent SFMs— gestures	28.6	21.4	7.1	4.8	4.8	4.8	7.1	9.6	7.1	2.4	2.4

Table 4.7 Mean duration (in seconds) of the delay between gestures and the associated word, analysed by syntactic class, clause-position and clause length

(a) Syntactic class

	N	V	Adj.	Pron.	Prep.	Dem. Adj.
M_1	0.915	0.736	0.747	1.20	2.33	1.06
M_2	0.770	0.661	0.664	0.905	0.583	1.06

(b) Clause position (in words)

	1–2	3–4	5–6	7–8	8+
M_1	1.29	0.534	0.881	1.82	0.804
M_2	0.737	0.393	0.672	1.22	0.746

(c) Clause length (in words)

	1–4	5–8	9–12	13–16	17+
M_1	0.498	0.868	0.744	0.810	1.26
M_2	0.498	0.706	0.650	0.540	0.990

M_1 = All gestures which show delay.
M_2 = M_1 + gestures which are initiated with or during the word.

DISCUSSION

A number of conclusions may be tentatively advanced. Firstly, there are two fundamentally distinct kinds of speech-focussed movement—gestures, and other speech-focussed movements. Secondly, the suggested distinction between the hesitant and the fluent phase, discussed in Chapter 3, receives further support from the distribution of equilibrium changes, and from the relative distribution of gestures observed. Thirdly, gestures appear to be by-products of lexical preplanning processes, and seem to indicate that the speaker knows in advance the semantic specification of the words he will utter; in some cases he has to delay to search for a relatively unavailable item. Some crude semantic specification of lexical items must therefore be part of the ideational planning process. Finally, lexical planning is a necessary, though not a sufficient condition for the occurrence of gestures.

One hypothesis that can be offered to account for the fact that gestures precede lexical items (rather than occur simultaneously with them) is that there is a greater repertoire of lexical items than of gestures to choose from. Lexical items have to be drawn from a large corpus – the mental lexicon probably consists of 20,000–30,000 items. Not all, of course, will be candidates at each choice point, some items will necessarily be excluded by the preceding linguistic context – but in some cases, the number of lexical items which satisfy the semantic and syntactic constraints will be large (these of course will be words of low transitional probability; that is to say, unpredictable in context). On the other hand, the repertoire of gestures typically employed in conversation is comparatively small. Hick's Law would therefore suggest that in the verbal medium, with a greater number of alternatives to choose from, selection of a lexical item should take longer than the selection of a gesture in the nonverbal medium.

Conclusion

This chapter reported some research into the interconnections in time between some aspects of nonverbal behaviour and spontaneous speech in conversation. It focussed on speaker eye-gaze and hand movement and gesture. It demonstrated that there are strong interconnections between the planning units underlying spontaneous speech (explored in detail in Chapter 3), as reflected in the patterns of hesitations, and the organization of these nonverbal forms of behaviour. Speaker eye-gaze is most common during the most fluent phases of spontaneous speech; and the most complex speaker hand gestures also tend to occur in these phases, although they often arise during the short

Table 4.8 Position in speech of changes in the basic equilibrium position of the arms and hands

	Number of changes in equilibrium position corresponding to each category	Number of occurrences of each phenomenon not accompanied by change in equilibrium position	G	Probability
End of hesitant phase	5	20	22.118	$p < 0.001$
End of fluent phase	8	20	39.336	$p < 0.001$
Clause juncture	24	180	61.448	$p < 0.001$
Other	14	1620	–	–

pauses which punctuate these otherwise fluent episodes. Pascal was certainly right — our nature does consist in motion, and what is interesting is that this motion is based around complex speech rhythms. Not rhythms of sound but of complex mental operations. Operations which result in, and are necessary for, the originality and the very spontaneity of spontaneous speech. Operations which guide and direct all other speaker activity.

The focus of the research so far has been on speech and nonverbal behaviour within a turn in conversation. Now we turn to the organization of conversations themselves. The cognitive rhythms which we have begun to map out will again be seen to play a crucial role. The most basic organizational principle underlying conversations is the turn-taking principle. There must be some means for participants to recognize when it is their turn to speak. But how is this done? What signals do speakers use to pass on the turn and how are these signals connected to the processes of planning and producing the spontaneous speech which makes up the conversation? In the next chapter we turn our attention to just such considerations.

Turn-taking in conversation

It is an impertinent and unreasonable fault in conversation for one man to take up all the discourse.

RICHARD STEELE
The *Spectator* (1711)

Introduction

In this book so far, we have concentrated on the organization of behaviour within a turn in conversation. Now we switch our attention to the organizational principles underlying the relationship between turns. In this chapter, we will consider the system of signals and rules which operate in conversation to regulate the process of turn-taking. In the next chapter we will consider a number of attempts to unravel the causes of (and significance of) those instances in which the turn-taking mechanism apparently breaks down, resulting in interruption.

One fundamental and apparently universal feature of conversation (see Miller 1963), is the fact that turn-taking does occur, that is:

(1) Speaker-change recurs, or at least occurs.
(2) Overwhelmingly, one party talks at a time.
(3) Occurrences of more than one party speaking simultaneously are common, but brief.
(4) Transitions (from one turn to the next) with no gap and no overlap are common. Together with transitions characterized by slight gap or slight overlap, they make up the vast majority of transitions.
(5) Turn order is not fixed, but varies.

(6) Turn size is not fixed, but varies.
(7) Length of conversation is not specified in advance.
(8) What parties say is not specified in advance.
(9) Relative distribution of turns is not specified in advance.
(10) Number of parties can vary.
(11) Talk can be continuous or discontinuous.

(from Sacks *et al.* 1974, pp. 700–1.)

All of this represents a considerable achievement. Conversations unfold in real time and yet parties to the conversation synchronize their turns – usually highly coherent and consistent with respect to topic – in a matter of milliseconds. Parties to the conversation comprehend speech, plan speech and synchronize with respect to each other in an apparently universal web of interaction. It is perhaps not surprising that turn-taking has attracted a good deal of research attention. Its roots have been sought in developmental psychology, its failure in clinical psychology and its theoretical basis in ethnomethodology, linguistics and psychology generally.

Models of turn-taking in conversation

The first point to stress about theoretical models of the turn-taking process in conversation is that there seem to be few points of contact between them. The models derived by those working within the theoretical framework of psychology and exemplified by the work of Kendon (1967), Duncan (1972) and Duncan and Fiske (1977) have concentrated on the role of nonverbal elements in turn-regulation (eye-gaze, gesture, etc.) and to the extent that they have considered language at all, they have considered aspects of language which can be analysed independently of the 'meaning' of the conversation. The linguistic elements in question would include syntax and intonation. These psychological accounts offer the observer high reliability of measurement in that the observer's task is to look for and analyse the presence of certain apparently independent features. The theoretical models derived by those working in disciplines outside psychology, on the other hand, have been very different. Here the concentration has been on language and the 'meaning' of the conversation. The best known theoretical model from a discipline other than psychology is that of Sacks, Schegloff and Jefferson (1974). Their account largely seems to ignore the role of nonverbal signals.

Psychologists such as Starkey Duncan have suggested that the turn-taking process can be entirely accounted for by postulating a regulatory role for nonverbal and linguistic cues of a discrete and independent nature. In his model, none of these cues are proposed to carry greater weight than any other, nor are any recurrent cue clusters envisaged or proposed. Some of the cues identified by Duncan (1972) are part of the text (for example, completion of syntactic segments), some are nonverbal (such as completion of a gesture), but most are carried by the pitch, timing and intensity pattern of the speed. His cues in more detail are:

1. *Intonation*: rising or falling intonation pattern (the presence of intonation at phonemic clause boundaries characterized by a terminal juncture combination other than |22|, where |22| refers to a phonemic clause ending on a sustained intermediate pitch level (Trager and Smith 1951)).

2. *Drawl*: the presence of drawl on the final syllable, or on the stressed syllable of a terminal clause, where a terminal clause is defined by either rising or falling intonation.

3. *Sociocentric sequence*: the presence of one of several stereotyped expressions, typically following a substantive statement, such as 'you know', 'but uh' (etc.).

4. *Pitch/loudness*: a drop in paralinguistic pitch and/or loudness in conjunction with one of the sociocentric sequences. When used, these expressions typically followed a terminal clause, but did not often share the same paralanguage.

5. *Syntax*: the completion of a grammatical clause containing a subject−predicate combination.

6. *Gesture*: the termination of any hand gesticulation used during a speaking turn, or the relaxation of a tensed hand position during a turn, but excluding self and object adaptors (that is, self-touching movements or movements involving manipulation of objects).

Duncan's data base was a series of video recordings in which interactants knew that recordings were taking place. Duncan's model and other psychological accounts will be discussed in detail later on in this chapter.

The work of Sacks, Schegloff and Jefferson (1974) stands alongside that of Duncan as being one of the few attempts to systematize a general theory of turn-taking. Sacks *et al.* present a series of observations as to the temporal organization of conversation. The data base which these workers used in order to account for this organization consisted of audio-recordings of a variety of naturalistic conversations such as telephone calls and coffee-room encounters. These were transcribed with great attention to the temporal placement of utterances, but with rather less focus on intonation and paralinguistic features. No statistical evidence is presented; rather Sacks *et al.* present a series of examples to illustrate the principles involved. Whilst this may allow for considerable illumination of certain points, evidence as to the reliability of their observations and the frequency of occurrence of the phonomena is simply not available.

Two basic components are proposed by which turns at talk are firstly, recognizable as such, and secondly, allocated – the 'turn-constructional' and 'turn-allocational' components respectively. In constructing a turn, a speaker uses various unit-types which for English include sentential, clausal, phrasal and lexical constructions. By virtue of these units, any listener can make a projection of the unit-type being generated, and, it is proposed, anticipate its end point. Thus, if, in conversation, someone says: 'I think you're . . .', it is possible to predict that the next word would be 'right' or 'wrong', and that after this next word might be an appropriate point to reply. This projective ability is crucial to the turn-allocational system (and points towards highly developed psycholinguistic skills). It is considered that a speaker is initially entitled to one such unit, and that the boundary points described by their endings are suitable loci for a speaker-switch. They are therefore described as 'transition relevance places' and the 'transfer of speakership is coordinated by reference to such transition relevance places, which any unit type instance will reach' (Sacks *et al.*, p. 703).

The allocation of turns is achieved through three techniques, the 'preference' for which is hierarchically arranged. Thus the current speaker may choose the next speaker by using in their talk a 'current speaker selects next' technique, such as an addressed question ('Jack, what is the time?'). If this option is not used, other participants may self-select by beginning utterances of their own, the first person to speak up acquiring the turn. Finally, if none of these occurs, the previous speaker may (but need not) continue into another turn. A number of 'repair mechanisms' are described which come into operation when the system described above fails to coordinate participants. The most usual problem is multiple starts during self-selection, repaired by the cessation of speech by all bar one interactant.

In their account, Sacks *et al.* exploit the 'common-sense' knowledge about the basic pragmatics of language. The phenomenon of turn-taking exemplifies this feature of their work, in proposing that interactants begin, or attempt to begin, their next turn around possible transition relevance places rather than continuously or randomly throughout the conversation. Such points are considered to be 'projectable' by virtue of the listener's knowledge of the possible unit-types under construction. Thus Sacks *et al.* give the following examples (p. 721 – the symbol [indicates spontaneous speech):

Penny: An' the fact is I – is I jus thought it was so kind of stupid
       [I didn' even say anything [when I came home.
Janet: [Y–   [Eh–

and

Ken: I saw 'em last night [at uhmn school.
Jim: [They're a riot.

Sacks *et al.* argue that listeners are sensitive to, and able to predict, such 'possible completion points' through their knowledge of language (but also of course through their interpretation of specific intonational patterns). It is perhaps the very flexibility of the system, described in a decontextualized and idealized manner, that makes interpretation difficult. Sacks *et al.* cannot account for the actualization of one 'transition relevance place' over another, and whilst some reference is made to intonation as a guide to completion ('any word can be made into a "one-word" unit-type via intonation', p. 722), the system as described seems to rely on a set of criteria bound together largely by the reader's own linguistic intuitions.

Inspection of the examples of transition relevance places offered by Sacks *et al.* also suggests, that these are often constituted by clausal boundaries; as such these instances would correspond to the turn-yielding cue of clausal completion identified by Duncan. The favoured position of this 'cue' in the Sacks *et al.* system, however, would raise difficulties for the independence of this cue within Duncan's turn-yielding model.

An important feature of the concept of transition relevance is its ability to account for the location of interruptions. Jefferson (1973) suggests that where overlaps in speech arise, they may be seen to reflect the projection of 'transition relevance places' as in:

A: Uh you been down here before [havenche.
B: [Yeh.

(from Sacks *et al.*, p. 707)

The placement of turn-taking at transition relevance places allows for a minimal overlap, since these are points where a current speaker can or should exit. Such placement can be shown to demand a high degree of skill in the prediction of temporal patterning, as in:

a: The guy who doesn't run the race doesn't win it,
     but 'e doesn't lose it.

b: ⌈B't lose it.⌉

(from Jefferson 1973, p. 51)

These examples highlight a major theoretical difference between Sacks *et al.* and Duncan, since they suggest that interruption can be an orderly feature of the turn-taking system and, in addition, indicate that its production can sometimes be the product of considerable precision. Duncan, however, seems to consider interruption merely as a breakdown in the system. (We will return to this point in the next chapter.)

A major difficulty with the Sacks *et al.* model concerns the ability of listeners to recognize when the completion of a unit-type is not intended as a turn ending. Quite clearly, it cannot be appropriate to interject at all transition relevant locations, since such loci arise with a high frequency. Similarly, no information is contained within the description of listener self-selection by which speakers could indicate their intention or desire to continue speaking. Within the Duncan model, completion points are signalled through linguistic or nonverbal cues which are treated as equivalent in their informational power. The 'turn-yielding' cues which constitute the core of the model place the control of temporal patterning with the speaker, and display a theoretically primary concern with the achievement of smooth switching as a consequence. Whilst this emphasis permits some explication of such features as turn-maintenance and exchange, it places all interruptions into a category of erroneous interchanges for which the system can offer little internally consistent account.

Each model is capable therefore of providing some insights into the mechanisms of turn-taking, yet neither is really a sufficient account of the whole process. Both seem to have operated from a restricted data base (Duncan devised his model on the basis of two conversations; Sacks *et al.* studied a considerable number but without the benefits of video-recording) and through this to have achieved very different vantage points on the same phenomenon. Sacks *et al.* outline the rules but the role of specific features in local turn-management is ignored. Duncan concentrates on the specific features but does not discuss the general rules. The possibility that a partial synthesis between these may be achieved by consideration of both linguistic and nonverbal behaviours will be implicit in this chapter and the next.

But first let us consider the development of the process of turn-taking.

Development of turn-taking skills

The development of turn-taking in conversation can be traced through various stages from the earliest interactions between mothers and infants (Trevarthen 1977). The earliest vocal interactions between mothers and infants are dominated by periods of simultaneous vocalization, and this continues up to the second year of life (Anderson 1977). For example, vocalizations of 3-month-old infants are reported to occur twice as often when the mother is talking simultaneously with the infant, as when the mother is silent (Anderson and Vietze 1977). Such simultaneous vocalization usually terminates with the infant shifting to a listener role, while the mother continues to talk (Stern 1974; Stern *et al.* 1975). As the child develops, so too does his basic conversational skill (see Mayo and La France 1978). Welkowitz *et al.* (1976) observed significant convergence in the switching pauses of turn-taking in the case of 5½-year-olds. De Long (1974, 1975) observed the presence of turn-yielding cues in nursery school children − certain types of movements clustered around the ends of speaker turns. Since it has been observed that certain movements fulfil important regulatory functions in adult conversations it may be suggested that nursery school children have already acquired certain aspects of this skill.

Clinical aspects of turn-taking in conversation

Despite the universal status of turn-taking, and the fact that it can be traced to conversations involving fairly young chidren, it may nevertheless appropriately be thought of as a skill. Skills are learned behaviours which improve with practice and feedback and which some people perform better than others (Argyle and Kendon 1967, Argyle 1974). There is a considerable body of evidence to suggest that certain clinical groups are poor at performing this particular skill. The evidence to suggest that schizophrenics are poor at synchronizing speech in conversation is based on observations of clinical interviews, especially standardized clinical interviews (Chapple and Lindemann 1942; Matarazzo and Saslow 1961). This technique involves the interviewer varying his behaviour in a systematic fashion throughout the interview − in some periods, confining his comments to a short duration; in others behaving in a non-directive fashion; and in others placing the interviewee in a mildly stressful situation by remaining silent or interrupting. In this situation, psychiatrically normal individuals use longer and fewer speaker-turns than schizophrenics. When an 'adjustment score' is computed (an algebraic measure of the subject's duration of interruption of the interviewer minus his duration of failure to respond), it is found that, for normals, this score is essentially zero, whereas for schizophrenics it is typically negative, and fairly high. This means that, in conversation, normals interrupt and fail to respond to the interviewer in about equal amounts (and, in fact, they do little of either) whereas schizophrenics typically fail to respond for much longer periods than they interrupt. Chapple, in fact, has stated that this negative adjustment score is one of the most characteristic diagnostic features in schizophrenia. Schizophrenics either do not appear to see the signals telling them when to talk in conversation or they are failing to interpret them. The former suggestion is supported by the accumulated evidence which suggests that schizophrenics display grossly aberrant gaze behaviour in conversation with extremely low levels of gaze at their interlocutor (Riemer 1949, 1955; Lefcourt *et al.* 1967; Argyle and Kendon, unpublished, cited by Argyle 1967; Rutter and Stephenson 1972). However, such evidence has been seriously questioned by Rutter (1973) who has demonstrated the methodological inadequacy of most of these early studies. Rutter went on to investigate the gaze behaviour and turn-taking skills of schizophrenics in free conversation with other schizophrenics and with psychiatrically normal partners. His series of studies demonstrated firstly that in terms of overall measures of gaze, schizophrenics behave very similarly to normals (Rutter 1976), and secondly, that in terms of gaze patterning, the two groups are also very similar (Rutter 1978). He also found no significant differences in measures of turn-taking skill in both groups — schizophrenics actually spent less time in simultaneous speech (one of the most frequently used indices of conversational breakdown) than some of the control groups (Rutter 1977a). It has thus been suggested by Rutter that the typical poor performance of schizophrenics in turn-taking skills may be confined to clinical interviews on personal matters (Rutter 1977a, 1977b).

It is, of course, also possible that schizophrenics would display normal patterns of gaze behaviour in conversation, and yet still show poor performance at synchronizing speech. That is to say, some groups of schizophrenics may have some difficulty in interpreting conversational signals. There is little data bearing on this. However, La Russo (1978) has demonstrated that paranoid schizophrenics are more sensitive than normals to genuine nonverbal facial cues (which communicate a particular stress or relief from stress). Whether this result would obtain with other categories of schizophrenia is not clear, because, as La Russo notes, paranoids suffer least impairment of intellectual functioning (Ginett and Moran, 1964; Moran *et al.* 1960), and are the most cooperative group to work with (Turner 1964). The more general question of the accuracy of interpretation by schizophrenics of other types of nonverbal signal remains unanswered.

Other groups, apart from schizophrenics, with a variety of clinical diagnoses, are also thought to lack adequate social skills, including turn-taking skills. As Trower *et al.* (1978) point out, failure of social competence, leading to rejection and social isolation, may be a primary cause of many clinical problems, and, they argue, certain clinical problems may improve as a result of training in social skills. Trower *et al.* (1978) carried out a survey of a group of patients diagnosed as having neuroses and personality disorders. They compared specific elements of social behaviour of a group of these individuals judged to be socially competent (by two psychologists and two psychiatrists), with a group of patients whom, the judges all agreed, were socially unskilled. The two groups differed on most of the behavioural elements assessed and also on the 'handing over of conversation' element. Trower *et al.* describe the characteristics of the socially unskilled group: 'Their speech lacked continuity and was punctuated with too many silences; they failed to hand over to take up the conversation and generally, did little or nothing to control the interaction, leaving the other person to make all the moves' (Trower *et al.* 1978, p. 50). A variety of treatment procedures have been devised to train social skills (Marzillier and Winter 1978; Trower *et al.* 1978).

Psychological studies of turn-taking (1): the 'traffic signal' approach

I want to argue that the earliest studies in psychology on how participants managed to regulate conversation were based on an implicit 'traffic signal' conceptual framework – the signals used to regulate conversation were thought to possess universal significance and were obligatory in their operation (see also Beattie 1980a) and were nonverbal in nature. Kendon (1967) compared the listener's (q's) response to the speaker (p), when p ended his utterance with or without gaze. Listener responses were categorized 'q fails to respond, or pauses before responding' and 'q responds without a pause'. Kendon observed that if the utterance terminated with speaker gaze, listeners were more likely to respond without a pause than if it did not. In subsequent interpretations of this study, speaker gaze seems to have been regarded like a traffic signal telling listeners when to respond – 'floor apportionment is also requested by eye movements which act as signals of a speaker's intention' (Argyle 1974, p. 202). Of course, gaze was not as efficient as a traffic signal in that there were a number of instances in the Kendon study when the signal did not come on and when the listener set off immediately (29.3% of all immediate listener responses followed utterances terminating without speaker gaze). Moreover, in some cases, when the light turned green the listener failed to move off. This 'traffic light' approach has found its way into the clinical literature. Thus, one treatment which Trower *et al.* (1978) suggest for poor turn-taking skills in conversation is 'ask the other a question and continue looking at him, this may include leaning forward'. Marzillier and Winter (1978) also report a treatment procedure used with a patient whose 'speech was characterised by long, boring monologues punctuated by frequent hesitations and repetitions with little or no attempt to involve the other person' (p. 69). Their treatment consisted of encouraging him to ask more questions. In both cases, the patient was encouraged to turn on the traffic lights. If this mechanism failed, the fault must lie with his fellow interactants.

Other observational studies have suggested that different behaviours may perform a similar floor-apportionment function. De Long (1974, 1975) found an increase in certain types of kinesic activity towards the ends of utterances, in the case of nursery school children, although Wiemann, cited by Wiemann and Knapp (1975) did not find an increase in any form of behaviour, except speaker gaze towards the ends of utterances, in the case of adults. These studies are, however, less direct than that of Kendon, because they did not consider the relationship between the occurrence of any of these behaviours and the efficiency or speed of the turn-taking process. Subsequent attempts to test the main line of evidence for the hypothesis that speaker gaze acts as a regulatory signal in conversation, have produced conflicting results. I investigated the relationship between the presence of speaker gaze at the ends of utterances and the durations of the succeeding switching-pauses in samples of supervisions recorded at the University of Cambridge (Beattie 1978a). The hypothesis under test was that if gaze does perform a regulatory function, as Kendon suggested, speaker gaze at the ends of syntactically and intonationally complete utterances should reduce the speaker-switch latency. It is, of course, necessary to consider only complete utterances in a test of this hypothesis, in order to exclude interruptions; that is to say, speaker-switches where the current speaker had not intended to relinquish the floor, and where his utterance is not intonationally complete. The results obtained in this study revealed that speaker gaze did not significantly reduce the length of the succeeding switching-pause, as was predicted. Elzinga (1978a, 1978b) obtained confirmatory evidence for a floor-apportionment function for gaze for English-speakers, but not for Japanese-speakers. Rutter *et al.* (1978) produced partially confirmatory evidence in the case of conversations between strangers but not in the case of conversations between friends. Clearly there are a number of highly complex social variables which seem to interfere with the effectiveness of this particular set of traffic lights. One may, in fact, harbour doubts on the basis of these studies on whether this green light is as universal a signal as was once claimed.

The alternative methodology to these observational studies was an experimental one and involved the removal of visual signals. In a sense, this is analogous to attempting to determine the effectiveness of traffic lights simply by turning them off and observing the inevitable chaos. Thus, a number of studies have looked at the temporal structure of conversations in sound-only conditions, in which inter-actants were either separated by some physical barrier (Jaffe and Feldstein 1970; Cook and Lalljee 1972; Butterworth *et al.* 1977; Rutter and Stephenson 1977), or were conversing by (simulated) telephone (Kasl and Mahl 1965; Butterworth *et al.* 1977). These studies have, however, generally concluded that conversation is in no way disrupted in sound-only conditions. The actual measures they employed can be criticized on a number of grounds (see Beattie 1981a). For example, all of these studies, with the exception of Kasl and Mahl 1965, have considered frequency of interruption as a crucial index of possible regulatory chaos and all have defined this variable solely on the basis of the occurrence or non-occurrence of simultaneous speech (Butterworth *et al.* appear to employ a rather more accurate definition, but see Beattie 1981a). This definition is inadequate because a number of instances of simultaneous speech do not constitute simultaneous claimings of the turn and are, therefore, not interruptions in any ordinary sense. Duncan (1972) identified a number of such instances − attention signals; sentence completions by the listener (see also Jefferson 1973); brief requests for clarification; and brief re-statements of the immediately preceding speaker's utterance. Moreover, some interruptions can occur without simul-taneous speech. Ferguson (1976, 1977) defined silent interruptions as speaker-switches in which the first speaker's utterance is incomplete but where there is no simultaneous speech. Thus, the definition of interruption used in these studies may be inadequate. One other measure used in these studies may also be inadequate. All of the studies considered possible verbal substitution in the absence of the visual signals. It has been suggested that filled pauses ('ah', 'er', 'um', etc.) in speech may perform a floor-holding function (Maclay and Osgood 1959; Ball 1975; Beattie 1977; but see Lalljee and Cook 1969; Cook and Lalljee 1972 for contradictory evidence). Ball (1975) found that filled pauses at the ends of utterances effectively delayed subjects' assumption of the floor in conversational dyads. Beattie (1977) demonstrated that filled pauses effectively reduced the probability of interruption, at least for a short period (up to 600 milliseconds), in natural conversation. If visual cues play a role in synchronizing conversation, filled pauses should increase in frequency in no-vision conditions. Changes in filled pause rate should, however, be compared to the overall incidence of unfilled pauses, since filled pauses are hypothesized to occur "in response to the cue of the speaker's own silence" (Maclay and Osgood 1959, p. 41). None of the studies controlled for this variable, however. Instead they have computed an 'Ah ratio' controlling for the number of words, which is not correct, given the original Maclay and Osgood hypothesis. Using this 'Ah ratio', the studies have tended to produce inconclusive results. Kasl and Mahl (1965) found a significantly higher filled pause rate in the telephone condition than in the face-to-face condition, but Cook and Lalljee (1972), Rutter and Stephenson (1977) and Butterworth *et al.* (1977) found no significant differences. Again, because of the basic inadequacy of the measure used, these results are highly inconclusive.

In a parallel approach to this problem, I, with Phil Barnard, attempted to determine whether telephone conversations are disrupted, not by looking at normal town driving where the traffic lights have been switched off (as all other studies have done), but by looking at the ability of drivers to cross intersections where traffic signals are never available, i.e. in natural telephone calls. In this study (Beattie and Barnard 1979), we analysed the switching-pauses, interruption rate (defined as simultaneous turn-claimings), and filled pause rate (controlled for unfilled pause rate) in natural directory enquiry calls.

The analysis of telephone calls

METHOD AND PROCEDURE

The conversations yielding the raw data for the study were sampled from a large corpus of directory enquiry conversations obtained by

Barnard (1974). The total corpus consists of more than 700 directory calls monitored at a trunk telephone exchange. The monitoring took place over a four-month period during the summer. In this period there were 18 monitoring sessions of one hour each. These sessions were distributed across the day shift and distributed across days of the week. The calls were monitored at a single switchboard position and all incoming calls to that position during each hour session were recorded on a cassette tape recorder. In all cases operators knew their conversations were being monitored. They were also aware that the monitoring was for research purposes only and was in no way to be used to assess their performance. The taped conversations were transcribed and no record of operator identity was maintained. The great majority of the class consisted of requests for the telephone numbers of business subscribers. This is consistent with the normal pattern for day shift where the percentage of enquiries for the numbers of residential subscribers ranges from 8% to 13% of the total (Post Office National Directory Enquiry Call Analysis Record No. 731, August 1974).

On the basis of the transcripts of this large corpus, a very much smaller number of conversations was selected for detailed analysis of their temporal structure. A representative sample of 18 calls was subjected to temporal analysis. These calls ranged from 28 words in length (subscriber 9, operator 19) to 492 words (subscriber 220, operator 272). The overall mean length of the 18 conversations was 115.8 words (subscriber 58.8, operator 57.0). Two examples of directory enquiry calls are presented below:

Example 1

Op 1	Directory Enquiries, for which town please?
	(0)
Sub 1	Letchworth, please
	(0)
Op 2	Letchworth, and the name of the people?
	(267)
Sub 2	Yes Anyname Cinema.★
	(467)
Op 3	Anyname Cinema/Letchworth 999999
	(467)
Sub 3	Letchworth 999999
	(0)
Op 4	Sright
	(0)

Sub 4　Goodbye
　　　　*Imaginary names and numbers are substituted for the
　　　　real ones in these examples.

Example 2
Op 1　Directory Enquiries, for which town please?
　　　　　(400)
Sub 1　Woburn Sands
　　　　　(800)
Op 2　Woburn Sands. Yes.
　　　　　(1067)
Sub 2　And the name is Anyname.
　　　　　(1067)
Op 3　The name of the person is Anyname?
　　　　　(0)
Sub 3　Anyname, yes.
　　　　　(8400)
Op 4　What initials please?
　　　　　(800)
Sub 4　A.B.
　　　　　(2800)
Op 5　A.B. / is it Wood Place? // Apsley Guise?
Sub 5　Er
　　　　　(1000)
Sub 6　Apsley Guise that's right // Wood Place.
Op 6　Yes
　　　　　(467)
Op 7　It's Woburn Sands 9999
　　　　　(800)
Sub 7　9999 er now / um is, there's not been any change of
　　　　coding or anything like that about that number?
　　　　　(1000)
Op 8　Just checking for you. / I've got a list of changed numbers
　　　　but I don't think that's one of them. / No that's not on the
　　　　changed numbers list. / It should be alright.
　　　　　(400)
Sub 8　Well, I can't get it. I've just tried it.
　　　　　(467)
Op 9　Have you? // Well I should dial 100 and ask the operator
　　　　to help you.
Sub 9　Yeah.
　　　　　(1000)
Sub 10　Err well / I see. Who will know if there is any change

of / ah exchange um and all the rest of it?

    (0)

Op 10   Well you know I've got the changed number list for Woburn Sands so it / um.

    (2733)

Sub 11 And it's definitely not one of them?

    (400)

Op 11   No it isn't. / No.

    (1067)

Sub 12 Ah the thing is this. Bit of a mystery. I've been trying this number for two days. / // Um yesterday somebody told me to put 58 in front of it / which got me a very unusual dialling / situation. / I haven't been able to get through and I'm you know. I have a letter from a large company saying he's there waiting for me to phone, and I can't get through.

Op 12   Yes.

    (1867)

Op 13   Yes, well, 58 should be put in front of some numbers but these these um / let me just read this / You've tried it with 58 in front?

    (0)

Sub 13 Yes.

    (6000)

Op 14   Oh, I should dial 100 and ask the operator to help you then because um / you know if you dial it with 58 in front it should certainly be alright.

    (667)

Sub 14 But I should be able to dial it without the 58 in front?

    (10667)

Op 15   Just a moment let me read this list here properly. No, you should have the 58 in front of it.

    (400)

Sub 15 I should have a ⎰ 58 in front.

             ⎱Yes yes and

Op 16   I'll just check the code for you while you're on the line. Perhaps it's the code you see. / Your code should be 0908.

    (800)

Sub 16 Yes, that's what I've been dialling.

    (1000)

Op 17   And / then 58 and then the number. / That should definitely be alright.

    (0)

Sub 17   Yes, I I've got a feeling there's something going on, on the exchange there, because it gives a very funny, very sort of, you know, it dials, then it stops.
(1667)

Op 18   Oh ⎰ that sounds like
Sub 18   ⎱ And then it
goes on again
(800)

Op 19   That sounds like a fault on the phone itself / not on, not on any dialling. If you're actually getting a ringing tone it should be alright. It's a ⎰ faul-
⎱who do
Sub 19   I get on to about fault enquiries anyway?
(1067)

Op 20   Fault / enquiries, or or / eh dial 100 and ask the operator to help you and she'll report it.
(1667)

Sub 20   Yes, O.K., then.
(200)

Op 21   One or the other. 191 is faults if you would prefer to go through them.
(933)

Sub 21   Alright, thank you very much indeed.
(0)

Op 22   Goodbye.
(0)

Sub 22   Bye Bye.

Symbols used in transcription are as follows (adapted from Schegloff and Sacks 1973):
/   indicates unfilled pause ⩾ 200 milliseconds.
//   indicates point at which following utterance interrupts.
(x) indicates switching pause of x milliseconds.
{   indicates simultaneous speech.

Example 1 represents an almost optimal exchange in which the subscriber receives the desired number with minimal discussion. Only 17 words are spoken by the operator (in addition to the number) and seven by the subscriber. Example 2 is a much longer conversation resulting from the subscriber's failure to get an answer from a certain number and therefore checking that he was in fact dialling the correct number. These two examples should give some idea of the range in length of directory enquiry calls. The conversations involved 18 different subscribers and each call was 'handled' in the exchange by one of four operators in the present sample.

The temporal aspects of each conversation were analysed using an Ediswan pen oscillograph and pause detector. For the purpose of the present analysis an unfilled pause was defined as a silent period $\geqslant 200$ milliseconds. Filled pauses were identified by the presence of a filler such as 'um', 'er', 'ah', etc.

For the sake of comparison, data obtained on the temporal structure of natural face-to-face conversations are included. These face-to-face conversations were university supervisions or seminars (as in Chapter 4).

RESULTS

Temporal structure of conversations
The initial analyses were directed at establishing the basic temporal characteristics of switches between the operator talking and the subscriber talking and vice versa. The mean (and median) length of switching-pause in cases where the operator yielded the floor to the subscriber (operator—subscriber) and in cases where the subscriber yielded the floor to the operator (subscriber—operator), were 507 (median = 400) and 474 milliseconds (median = 333 milliseconds) respectively.

In calculating mean (and median) switching-pauses it should be noted that question—answer pairs are excluded as are those switching-pauses requiring the accessing of written information, almost invariably by the operator, e.g. the switching-pause of 8.4 seconds preceding operator four in Example 2. In this study short attentional signals (e.g. operator six, Example 2) are not regarded as speaker-turns and therefore the delay before their production is not taken into consideration in the calculation of the mean switching-pause for a conversation. Non-parametric statistical analysis showed that the difference in delay for operator—subscriber and subscriber—operator switches was not significant (Mann–Whitney U test, $z = 0.626$, $n_1 = 58$, $n_2 = 88$, p 0.53; two-tailed test). These results from the telephone contrast with a mean of 575 milliseconds (median = 360 milliseconds) delay obtained for comparable speaker switches in natural face-to-face conversation (Beattie 1978a) again excluding the delay preceding responses to questions. There was no significant difference in speaker-switch times in face-to-face and telephone conversations (Mann–Whitney U test, $z = 0.683$, $n_1 = 117$, $n_2 = 146$, p 0.50; two-tailed test). However these results must be interpreted cautiously in the light of the difference in the topic of conversations studied.

The proportion of immediate speaker-switches (i.e. $\leqslant 200$ milliseconds duration) was also considered. The data for these immediate switches are given in Tables 5.1a and 5.1b, together with a figure for comparable face-to-face conversations (Beattie 1978a). Here the data are most appropriately expressed as a percentage of the total number of switches (again excluding question–answer pairs).

It can be seen from the tables that the percentages of immediate switches are essentially comparable for operator–subscriber and subscriber–operator switches and identical for telephone conversations and face-to-face interactions! There was no significant difference in the proportion of immediate speaker-switches between the telephone and face-to-face interactions ($G = 0,000; p > 0.05$; Sokal and Rohlf, 1973) or between operator–subscriber and subscriber–operator switches ($G = 0.018; p > 0.05$).

The remaining speaker-switches are those which involve simultaneous claimings of turn, a characteristic which is generally regarded as a breakdown of the conversation process (e.g. see Rutter and Stephenson 1977). The percentage of all speaker-switches involving simultaneous claimings of the turn is given in Tables 5.2a and 5.2b. It should be noted that the question–answer pairs are included in this

Table 5.1a The percentage of all speaker-switches which were immediate ($\leqslant 200$ milliseconds)

Telephone	Operator–Subscriber	34.5%
(DQ)	Subscriber–Operator	34.1%
	Both	34.2%
Face-to-face (Beattie, 1978a)		34.2%

Table 5.1b The number of immediate ($\leqslant 200$ milliseconds) and non-immediate (> 200 millisecond) speaker-switches

		immediate	non-immediate
Telephone	Operator–Subscriber	20	38
(DQ)	Subscriber–Operator	30	58
	Both	50	96
Face-to-face (Beattie, 1978a)		40	77

Table 5.2a Percentage of all speaker-switches involving simultaneous claimings of the turn (including question—answer pairs)

Telephone (DQ)	Op—Sub	6.7%
	Sub—Op	5.7%
	Both	6.3%
Face-to-face	F to F (without speaker gaze at end of utterance)	14.1%
	F to F (with gaze at end of utterance)	7.1%
	Both	10.6%

Table 5.2b Number of smooth speaker-switches and switches involving simultaneous claimings of the turn

		Smooth	Sim. turn-claiming
Telephone (DQ)	Op—Sub	126	9
	Sub—Op	99	6
	Both	225	15
Face-to-face	F to F (without speaker gaze at end of utterance)	73	12
	F to F (with gaze at end of utterance)	78	6
	Both	151	18

analysis (this has the effect, of course, of substantially increasing the numbers involved). Once again the data from the present study are contrasted with data from face-to-face interactions. Here the face-to-face data include a comparison involving speaker gaze. The important contrasts to emerge from these data are, first, that the percentage of simultaneous claimings of the turn obtained from the telephone conversations is rather lower than the overall percentage for face-to-face conversations. The difference is not, however, significant ($G = 2.544$, $p > 0.05$). Indeed, the telephone results are closer to face-to-face switches involving gaze than to those not involving gaze. However, speaker gaze at the end of utterances does not significantly decrease the probability of simultaneous turn-claiming in face-to-face interaction (G = 1.508, $p > 0.05$). Second, the percentage of simultaneous claiming of the turn does not differentiate between subscriber–operator and operator–subscriber switches. There is no significant difference in the relative number of subscriber–operator and operator–subscriber switches involving simultaneous claimings of the turn (G = 0.092, $p > 0.05$). The fact that there is no significant difference in the relative incidence of simultaneous turn-claiming in face-to-face and telephone conversations, and moreover that a higher proportion of speaker-switches involving simultaneous speech seem to occur in face-to-face interactions, strongly suggests that natural telephone conversations need not lead to an increased incidence of breakdowns in a transition from speaker to speaker. The duration of simultaneous speech occurring at switching points is given in Table 5.3. Although the duration of simultaneous speech is somewhat longer in the telephone conversations than in the face-to-face conversations the difference was not statistically reliable (U = 98, $n_1 = 15$, $n_2 = 18$, $p > 0.1$; two-tailed).

On the basis of the present data there is therefore no evidence that the absence of visual information adversely affects the management of transitions from speaker to speaker. Indeed, the bulk of the data presented in Tables 5.1 to 5.3 indicates that smooth transitions on the telephone are the rule rather than the exception. The basic temporal characteristics of speaker-switches on the telephone are at least comparable with those of face-to-face interaction. In fact, in terms of the overall delay involved, the data suggest that speaker-switching (for the types of switching considered) is plausibly executed faster on the telephone, although the differences have been non-significant. Furthermore, there is no evidence that experience influences the pattern of such switching in that operators and subscribers do not appear to differ significantly. The issue of whether or not specific verbal cues are used to compensate for the absence of a visual channel is taken up in the following analyses of the switching-pauses.

Table 5.3 Mean duration of simultaneous claimings of the turn (milliseconds)

Telephone (DQ)	Face-to-Face
627 ($n = 15$)	454 ($n = 18$)

Filled and unfilled pauses

If, as Maclay and Osgood (1959) propose, filled pauses act as verbal signals aimed at inhibiting potential interruption, then they should be emitted following unfilled pauses. In order to assess the potential contribution of filled pauses, the base rate of unfilled pauses was taken into account, and the ratio of filled to unfilled pauses computed. This ratio was computed for all participants who displayed unfilled and filled pauses (a few did not make use of both UPs and FPs). The resultant ratios are presented in Table 5.4. Statistical analysis using the non-parametric Mann–Whitney test showed that the ratios for the telephone participants were reliably higher than comparable ratios obtained by Beattie (1977) in face-to-face conversations ($U = 14$, $n_1 = 6$, $n_2 = 19$, $p < 0.02$; two-tailed test). In spite of the potential

Table 5.4 FP/UP ratios for participants in natural face-to-face and natural telephone conversations (includes both operators and subscribers but excludes three subscribers who did not display any UPs or FPs)

Face-to-face (Beattie 1977)	Telephone (DQ)	
	$\propto$	
0.139	0.625	
0.112	0.500	
0.123	1.200	
0.143	1.000	
0.156	1.000	
0.229	0.526	
	0.091	Subscribers
	0.333	
Mean = 0.150	0.182	
	1.500	
	0.200	
	0.750	
	0.750	
	0.333	
	0.556	
	0	Operators
	0.667	
	0.330	
	Mean = 0.586*	

*excluding one subscriber who used FPs but no UPs and thus had an FP/UP ratio of ∞.

contribution of factors associated with differences in the topics of the telephone and face-to-face conversations, these data indicate strongly that participants in telephone conversations employ filled pauses as a means of maintaining conversational control to a greater extent than do participants in face-to-face conversations. Additionally, the FP/UP ratios were separately analysed for operators and subscribers. The mean ratios are presented in Table 5.5. Statistical analysis showed that the ratios did not differ reliably between operators and subscribers ($U = 18$, $n_1 = 4$, $n_2 = 15$, $p > 0.1$; two-tailed test). However, the number of operators involved in this analysis is very small. There was, nevertheless, some indication of differential usage of filled pauses by operators and subscribers. When filled pauses were considered at the *beginnings* of utterances there was a substantial difference between operators and subscribers in terms of their frequency of using this verbal cue. The 18 subscribers emitted a total of 26 filled pauses at the beginnings of utterances, 55.3% of all FPs displayed, 21 of these occurred at the start of the response to a question from the operator. The corresponding figure for the operators was zero. Thus subscribers were significantly more likely to display FPs at the beginnings of utterances than elsewhere compared with operators ($G = 8.668$, $p < 0.01$).

Table 5.5 Mean FP/UP ratios for operators and subscribers †

	Subscribers	Operators
Mean FP/UP ratio	0.642	0.389
	($n = 14$)	($n = 4$)

† These data exclude those not displaying UPs or FPs; and FP/UP ratio of ∞, when FPs but no UPs appeared.

Finally, two correlational analyses were carried out to examine the relationship between switching-pauses and within-turn temporal structure. Conversations characteristically involving short duration switching-pauses should also be associated with shorter unfilled pauses prior to filled pauses, since the speaker will have to take rapid measures to fend off potential interruptions. With conversations involving longer switching pauses there would be less pressure to emit fillers such as 'um' and 'er'. In consequence, there should be a positive correlation between the mean time for speaker-switches and the mean length of unfilled pauses preceeding filled pauses. A Spearman test showed that there was indeed a significant positive correlation between these variables ($r_s = 0.54$, $p < 0.05$, see Table 5.6). This latter analysis refers to subscribers only ($n = 15$), since on only two

Table 5.6 Speaker switching-pauses and the temporal structure of utterances within the conversation (subscribers only) †

Subscribers	Mean switching pause within conversation milliseconds)	Mean length of UP preceding an FP (milliseconds)	FP/UP Ratio (milliseconds)
S1	1176	360	0.625
S2	300	0	0.500
S3	543	200	1.200
S4	478	200	1.000
S5	356	0	1.000
S6	558	600	0.526
S7	200	0	0.091
S8	0	0	0.333
S9	520	300	0.182
S10	0	0	∞
S11	456	0	1.500
S12	500	0	0.200
S13	289	190	0.750
S14	267	267	0.750
S15	750	0	0.333

† This table excludes three conversations in which subscribers did not display any UPs or FPs.

occasions in the case of operators were filled pauses directly preceded by unfilled pauses. This significant correlation is consistent with the results of a similar analysis of face-to-face interactions (Beattie 1977) and provides further support for the view that filled pauses play a part in fending off potential interruptions. However, on this view the ratio of filled to unfilled pauses might also be expected to be related to the length of the pause preceding an interruption, a relationship of this type was not found in the present data ($r_s = -0.16, n = 15, p > 0.1$).

The results of this study strongly suggest that the management of speaker-switching, as measured by the temporal characteristics of the transitions, is not impaired in natural telephone conversations. In short, visual cues to the viability of switching or interruption do not appear to constitute a necessary feature of adequate conversational management. There is, however, evidence that verbal cues, in the form of filled pauses, assume greater importance in the management of telephone conversations. Although there was some asymmetry in the use of these verbal signals between subscribers and operators, the vast majority of the measures indicate that operators and subscribers are behaving very similarly in terms of the temporal characteristics of switching. It must, of course, be acknowledged that directory enquiry conversations are highly structured and partially planned dialogues. Nevertheless, this comparability between the switching patterns of operators and subscribers tentatively suggests that the mass of accumulated experience possessed by the operator does not substantially modify the basic temporal course of certain kinds of transitions between speakers in natural telephone conversations.

The telephone study suggests that the 'traffic signal' explanation of turn-taking – that turn-taking is accomplished by nonverbal signals (such as eye-gaze) which are obligatory in their operation – is not correct.

Psychological studies of turn-taking (2): Duncan's approach

A different approach to the traffic signal paradigm described in the last section has been pioneered by Starkey Duncan (1972, 1973, 1974, 1975; Duncan and Fiske 1977). I want to suggest that this is (with some imagination) analogous to a driver wishing to move from a side road onto a main road during the rush-hour. There is no single universally understood signal which tells him when to move forward (there are no traffic lights at the intersection); rather there are a number of phenomena to which he must attend; the spacing of the cars on the main road, their speed, and their willingness to allow him to join the stream. On some occasions, the driver on the side road nudges forward, and drivers in the main stream wave him on. On other occasions they do not. The driver's chances of getting into the main stream of traffic are affected by all these variables (and probably more besides). Duncan (1972) identified six such cues in spontaneous conversation which seem to affect the probability of a listener taking the floor without any scrape (simultaneous turn-claimings). These turn-yielding signals involve verbal cues (clause completion, socio-centric sequences, e.g. 'you know'), intonational cues (rising or falling intonation, drawl on final syllables, drop in loudness and/or pitch in sociocentric sequences) and one nonverbal cue (gesture termination). He also identified one cue which can prevent a turn-taking attempt (the continuation of a hand or arm gesture). Duncan analysed the relationship between the conjoint occurrence of these turn-yielding cues in speech and the probability of listener turn-taking attempts, and he observed that in the absence of speaker-gesticulation 'the correlation between number of turn-yielding cues displayed and percentage of auditor turn-taking attempts was 0.96' (1972, p. 289). No smooth speaker-switches seemed to occur in the absence of one or more of these turn-yielding cues. The display of one or more of these cues also led to a significant reduction in the probability of simultaneous claimings of the turn. On the other hand, when the speaker was engaged in gesticulation, the incidence of listener turn-taking attempts fell virtually to zero. Thus, Duncan's analytic framework seems to predict rather well the behaviour of speakers and listeners in conversation with respect to its regulation. It differs from the traffic signal approach in that it does not focus upon one single signal, but on a set of features which can co-occur. Moreover, the response to these features is not obligatory, but optional: 'the auditor is not obliged to take a speaking turn in response to a regular turn-yielding signal by the speaker. The auditor may alternatively communicate in the back channel (that is say something such as "yeah", without claiming the floor (Yngve 1970)), or remain silent' (1972, p. 286). At least some of the signals discussed in the earlier framework carry obligatory responses. Trower *et al.* (1978) and Marzillier and Winter (1978) recommend that their patients asked questions because presumably questions require answers.

A similar approach to that of Duncan has been devised by Robbins *et al.* (1978), who have explored combinations of speaker verbal and nonverbal behaviours in much larger samples of speech than Duncan (Duncan only used two 19-minute conversations, involving three different speakers in his original study). Robbins *et al.* have investigated 30 different speakers; they have attempted to interpret the significance of different combinations of nonverbal behaviour (speaker gaze towards or away from the listener), pauses (either filled or unfilled), and intonational features (such as tonal inflection – open/closed). Unfortunately, they do not present any statistical evidence relating the various combinations of features to listener responses, and so in the following critique I will concentrate on Duncan's more direct approach.

Duncan's work seems to have a number of shortcomings. Firstly, Duncan provides information about only the gross efficiency of the turn-taking mechanism, that is, about the relationship between number of cues and the relative incidences of listener turn-taking attempts (and about the relative probabilities of these attempts resulting in simultaneous claimings of the turn). He provides no information on individual cues; thus the relative importance of any given cue (for example drawl or gesture) cannot be assessed. Moreover, no information is provided about the magnitude of speaker-switching pauses (i.e. whether they are long or short). It is thus not possible to assess how such cues might accelerate turn-taking in conversation.

Another problem with Duncan's study concerns the correlation between 'number of turn-yielding cues displayed' and 'percentage of auditor turn-taking attempts'. This was computed by dividing the 'number of auditor turn-taking attempts' by the 'frequency of display' of the relative number of turn-yielding cues. The correlation was found to be 0.96 ($p < 0.01$; 1-tailed test). However, only two instances of the simultaneous display of six turn-yielding cues were recorded. Thus the percentage of listener turn-taking attempts following the simultaneous display of six turn-yielding cues was calculated on the basis of an n of 2. Duncan observed that in one case out of two, a turn-taking attempt occurred; thus the percentage of such junctures accompanied by a turn-taking attempt was calculated to be 50%. If this one response had not occurred, the percentage of such junctures accompanied by a turn-taking attempt would have fallen from 50% to 0%! *This would have resulted in the correlation between percentage of listener turn-taking attempts and number of turn-yielding cues conjointly displayed falling from 0.96 to $r_s = 0.21$ ($p > 0.05$).* Thus, the overall conclusions seem to critically depend upon the occurrence of one response by the listener! Thus the effect cannot be considered statistically reliable.

Duncan's research, of course, depends upon the ability of judges to detect drawl and to score pitch and the other intonational features he discusses. In the early papers (1972, 1973, 1974, 1975), inter-observer reliabilities, that is, agreement between observers in scoring intonational features, are not reported. However, Duncan and Fiske (1977, pp. 341–2) do report inter-observer reliabilities for some nonverbal features (gaze direction, head nods, gesticulations) and intonational features (primary stress, phonemic clause boundaries, and deviations from the sustained intonation pattern). But no reliability checks were performed on clause completion, sociocentric sequences, paralanguage of sociocentric sequences, and drawl. Inter-observer reliabilities for the intonational features scored were very high, ranging between 85.7% (for scoring phonemic clause boundaries) to 94.2% (for scoring stress). These results, however, contrast markedly with those of Lieberman (1965, p. 52), who used the same basic system for scoring intonation – the Trager–Smith system – and found that 'when two competent linguists independently transcribe a set of sentences 60 per cent of the pitch levels and junctures of the two Trager–Smith transcriptions vary'. Some linguists have felt that the Trager–Smith system is very unreliable, but Duncan does not seem to have encountered this problem.

Turn-taking in conversation: a test of Duncan's model

Duncan's model of the turn-taking process needs to be tested. How crucial are the verbal and nonverbal signals he identified in controlling the exchange of the speaker role? Is it simply the number of cues that is important, as he suggested, or are some cues more important than others? Which cues are most commonly associated with the smooth exchange of turns in conversations? Can we measure these features reliably?

PROCEDURE

The samples of conversation studied were six natural dyadic inter-actions involving 12 different speakers. Five were supervisions, that is dyadic tutorials involving a tutor and an undergraduate student. The remaining sample involved two participants of a seminar engaged in prolonged interaction solely with each other. These interactions were observed and recorded through a one-way screen using Sony video cameras. Two judges separately recorded the incidence of the six turn-yielding cues identified by Duncan at every speaker-switch. Only speaker-switches occurring at places where the speaker was not gesticulating (this of course acts as an attempt-suppression signal according to Duncan) were studied (the subset excluded was very small). Inter-observer reliability in detecting a change in pitch at the end of an utterance was 88.7%. Inter-observer reliability in detecting drawl, on either the final or the stressed syllable, was 81.48%. Inter-observer reliability in scoring sociocentric sequences (filled pauses and parenthetic remarks) was 100%; clause completion, 98.3%; and a drop in pitch and/or loudness in conjunction with a sociocentric sequence, 92.1%.

RESULTS

In the present corpus, totalling 174 minutes, there were 230 speaker-switches, 214 smooth speaker-switches (i.e. not involving simultaneous claimings of the turn) and 16 non-smooth transitions.

It was observed in the present corpus that 13.55% of all smooth speaker-switches occurred in the absence of any turn-yielding cues (Duncan did not observe any, see Table 5.7).

The cue most frequently associated with speaker-switching (and therefore the most significant) was syntactic clause completion, involved in 61.30% of all switches (in which some turn-yielding cues were implicated). Clause completion at the ends of utterances tended

Table 5.7 Relationship between number of turn-yielding cues conjointly displayed and speaker-switching (the data from Duncan 1972 is included for comparison)
(No attempt-suppression signal displayed)

Number of turn-yielding cues conjointly displayed	Frequency of speaker-switching at junctures with different number of cues displayed		Simultaneous turns resulting from turn-taking attempt	
		(Duncan 1972)		(Duncan 1972)
0	41	(5)	12	(5)
1	22	(12)	2	(2)
2	23	(25)	0	(2)
3	108	(29)	2	(2)
4	36	(15)	0	(0)
5	0	(4)	0	0
6	0	(1)	0	0
	230	(91)	16	(11)

to be accompanied by a change in pitch level and (less often) by drawl on the final syllable. A change in pitch level occurred in 95.03% of speaker-switches preceded by clause completion. Only 2.60% of speaker-switches followed clause completion in isolation from intonational turn-yielding cues.

In contrast, the visual nonverbal turn-yielding cue (gesture termination) was implicated in only 8.70% of all smooth speaker-switches. There were pronounced individual differences in the speaker's usage of this cue — in the case of one speaker it was involved in 22.85% of all switches, in the case of two speakers it was not involved at all. Furthermore, 80.00% of speaker-switches involving this visual cue were also accompanied by clause completion. These results suggest that syntactic and accompanying intonational cues play the dominant roles in the regulation of turn-taking in conversation, and that visual nonverbal cues are much less significant.

It is interesting to note that the highest conjoint frequency of turn-yielding cues at a speaker-switch in the present study was three (and the most frequent combination of cues was clause completion, accompanied by a pitch change at the terminal juncture and drawl on the final or stressed syllable). In contrast, Duncan found little difference in the incidence of speaker-switches at locations occupied by two or three turn-yielding cues. Nevertheless, there was a significant correlation between the relative distribution of number of cues conjointly displayed at speaker-switches in the two studies (Spearman rank correlation coefficient, $r_s = 0.75$, $n = 7$, $p < 0.05$). The differences which arose between the two studies may be attributable to differences in dialect between the American subjects employed by Duncan and the British subjects employed in the present study. There is considerable evidence that differences in dialect do affect intonational features like pitch changes and drawl (see, for example, Tarone 1975; Crystal 1975). Drawl would appear to be particularly common and pronounced in middle-class non-American English dialects and thus may have been a more salient turn-yielding cue in the present study.

This study tended to lend support to the observations made by Duncan in 1972. The majority of smooth speaker-switches did involve one or more of the cues he identified. However, the results were not nearly so clear-cut as those of Duncan. He did not observe any smooth speaker-switches in the absence of one or more of these cues, but he observed 12 speaker-switches involving simultaneous turn-claimings at those points. In my follow-up study, however, I observed 29 smooth speaker-switches in the absence of turn-yielding cues – i.e. 13.6% of the total number of smooth switches. But the main theoretical point of departure from Duncan is the rejection of the linear model, outlined in detail in Duncan and Fiske (1977):

> We may begin by assuming that one participant is in the speaker state and the other participant is in the auditor state. Let us say that the transition readiness for each participant is represented by an ordinal scale readable by that participant. On this scale a high reading represents high transition readiness, and vice versa. Through periodic signal activation, the speaker can represent his current status on transition readiness. Specifically, through activating or not activating turn cues the speaker can indicate a point on the scale from zero to six (or whatever the maximum number of turn cues proves to be). Moreover, by activating the gesticulation signal, it appears that the speaker can indicate a zero value for transition readiness (regardless of concurrent turn-cue activation), or perhaps a negative one (p. 197).

This model has to be rejected because the linear correlation between number of cues and probability of a listener turn-taking attempt reported in Duncan (1972) was not replicated. The cues identified by Duncan are important, but important in that they operate in special cue combinations to define a possible turn transition point (compare the transition relevance places of Sacks *et al.*). Duncan seems to have successfully identified the cues implicit in the Sacks *et al.* framework whilst possibly building an erroneous model around them. In the next chapter, I will present more evidence from an analysis of political interviews which will lend further support to the conclusion that the cues identified by Duncan are crucial in conversation but that a model based on the notion of special cue combinations is the correct one.

Psychological studies of turn-taking (3): considering cognitive processes

I want now to introduce a third conceptual and metaphorical framework for looking at conversation. This is the one which I have found most useful. Consider the data on supervisions. Supervisions have a number of advantages as data for the study of conversation. In theoretical terms, speaker turns are highly variable (ranging from one word to sometimes over 15 minutes) making turn-taking complex and difficult. In practical terms, supervisions can be recorded in the laboratory with the minimum of experimenter contamination. They occur naturally in a university setting and, indeed, they occurred naturally in the room in which the video-recordings were made.

This research began by considering the cognitive processes under-lying spontaneous speech, in a conversational context (as in Chapter 3). There is considerable evidence that such cognitive processes are reflected in hesitation (Goldman-Eisler 1968), and the research began by investigating patterns in hesitation and phonation across time. Having begun by exploring production processes in spontaneous speech, I went on to determine the effects of these processes, and (as in Chapter 4) specifically temporal cycles, on the patterning of nonverbal behaviour in conversation. When I considered the distri-bution of speaker gaze with respect to temporal cycles, I found that it was organized in a loosely coordinated system with these cycles. It tended to be more common in the fluent phases than in the hesitant phases of the cycles, and extremely common at the clause junctures nearest the ends of the cycles (see Beattie 1978b for a detailed discussion). I also considered the relationship between the cycles and speaker movement and gesture, and found that the more complex iconic gestures seemed to originate in the pauses preceding the more uncommon lexical items in the fluent phases of the cycles (Butterworth and Beattie 1978). These gestures appear to be a by-product of lexical selection, since the pauses in which they originate are used for lexical search (Goldman-Eisler, 1958a, 1958b) and in addition, the form of the gesture is related to the word which follows. They thus would provide the listener with information about the interactional status of these pauses, i.e. they are pauses used for cognitive planning and not pauses purely designed to mark the end of a speaker turn. These observations would thus be compatible with Duncan's conclusions that the presence of gesture does act as an effective turn-suppression cue.

The main thrust of this work from the conversational viewpoint was to determine the effects of any patterns in the nonverbal behaviour (speaker gaze) on its operation as a turn-yielding signal (Beattie 1979b). To this end, 110 smooth speaker-switches were isolated, which followed speech segments that were syntactically and intonationally complete. These speaker-switches followed terminal utterances which occurred either in hesitant or fluent phases of temporal cycles. It was observed, as before, that speaker gaze did not generally reduce the switch latency, but it did seem to reduce the latency by a factor of 5 when it occurred at the end of turns in hesitant phases of temporal cycles (mean duration of switching-pause following a complete segment in hesitant phases of cycles accompanied by speaker gaze 378 milliseconds, compared with 1.918 seconds when unaccompanied by gaze). Thus, in this particular context, characterized by hesitation, and low levels of speaker gaze, when the single gaze cue does occur at the end of an intonationally complete speech segment, it does have a striking effect on the turn-taking process (see also Beattie 1980b). It is, of course, entirely sensible that the background patterning of the behaviour should affect its interactional function. In fact, one may suggest that the reason Kendon had originally observed a floor-apportionment function for this behaviour, was that he had studied conversations between pairs of Oxford undergraduates 'getting to know each other', in which the background level of gaze would have been low. In my attempted replication (Beattie 1978a), I studied supervisions, in which the interactants knew each other and in which the background level of gaze was much higher. One may, therefore, suggest that any such nonverbal behaviour will only possess important regulatory significance in conversations where the background level is low, and, moreover, its interactional significance will vary within a conversation as a function of this background level.

In other words, the scheme I am putting forward is one in which the driver has found himself on a road in which there are major repairs. The contractors have positioned a number of temporary road signs inscribed 'slow', 'temporary road surface', 'loose chippings', etc. along the route. The driver in the car has to take note of this information but, in addition, he has other work to do − he has to be careful to avoid workmen, plant machinery and other cars. He has to take note of the control panel in his car. Just as in conversation, the listener has difficult work to do in addition to timing his utterances carefully. He has to plan his utterances somewhat in advance of beginning to speak (Butterworth and Beattie 1978) and has to ensure that they are appropriate in context and cohesive with the preceding turn (Vuchinich 1977). I am therefore going to suggest that any single discrete sign on an otherwise clear road will have a greater effect on our driver's behaviour, than any discrete sign in the context of many others. Speaker gaze is an effective floor-apportionment signal only in a context of gaze aversion.

Conclusions

In this chapter, I have attempted to summarize a number of difficult theoretical accounts of turn-taking in conversation. Some of these accounts came from psychology and one came from ethnomethodology. I have tried to say something about the methodology underpinning the approaches as well as to detail the actual conclusions reached. The two most general theoretical models – those of Sacks *et al.* (1974) and Duncan (1972) – at first might seem incompatible but closer consideration reveals that they may be partially reconcilable. If, as I have suggested, we reject Duncan's linear model of turn-taking but nevertheless accept the cues he identified as being of major importance it is possible to see how combinations of these cues would constitute transition relevance places in the Sacks *et al.* framework. Sacks *et al.* devised a general model of turn-taking without filling in the low-level detail. Duncan described the low-level detail without considering some of the general principles involved.

Part of the reason for the enormous interest in turn-taking, at least within psychology of course, is because of its clinical relevance. Certain identifiable clinical groups are poor at performing this particular social skill. Each of the three psychological frameworks discussed seems to me to have different implications with respect to how social skills training procedures in this area should be implemented. So far, only the 'traffic light' approach has actually filtered through to the main stream of the clinical literature. The advice has been to 'turn on the green light' (question accompanied with gaze) and wait. The disadvantages of this approach are that firstly it does not appear to be that common in normal conversation (Beattie 1978a, found that only 22.5% of smooth speaker-switches in a sample of supervisions involved questions); and secondly, it makes a listener response obligatory, when, in most normal conversations, obligatory responding is not the norm. The Duncan framework, on the other hand, would recommend that the speaker's turn be marked by various intonational and nonverbal features which would provide the listener with a series of opportunities to take the floor, if he or she so desired. There are, of course, considerable grounds for training here. Interactants could be taught to segment their speech and vary their intonation in ways to make listener turn-taking attempts more probable. Furthermore, individuals could be taught that certain intonational features are open to different interpretations. Robbins *et al.* (1978) point out that there are class differences in the use and interpretations of certain critical intonational features. They note that the downward inflection of certain middle-class speakers is often viewed by working-class speakers as being overly assertive, and that the middle class often view the upward inflection of working-class speakers as indicative of extreme tentativeness and uncertainty. Duncan did not separate out the relative effectiveness of rising and falling intonation as turn-yielding cues, but undoubtedly, differences in effectiveness do exist. Moreover, given the class differences described by Robbins *et al.* with respect to these intonational features, one would predict that the efficacy of the cues will vary as a function of the target group. Social skills programmes could be devised to teach differences in interpretation of the various cues. The third framework, which I tentatively developed in this chapter, might lead to a programme in which interactants were taught to vary their nonverbal behaviours (such as gaze) systematically as they spoke, because it appears that only through systematic patterning can behaviours acquire their interactional significance. Nevertheless, there is clearly a need for more systematic research into this whole area before fully effective social skills training programmes can be developed.

Thus, unlike the earlier conceptual framework on turn-taking in conversation, which seems to recommend switching on a signal at the end of a speaker-turn after the interactant has decided to finish speaking, the other conceptual frameworks discussed in this chapter would seem to offer advice about how one should vary one's speech style, intonation and the accompanying nonverbal behaviours in conversation, in order to involve a second person. Only by varying the patterns of one's speech and accompanying nonverbal behaviour can interactants, it seems, fully weave their interlocutor into the fabric of their discourse.

Interruption in Conversation

Whoever interrupts the conversation of others to make a display of his fund of knowledge, makes notorious his own stock of ignorance.

SA'DI
'GULISTAN' (1258)

Introduction

Conversations appear to be remarkably orderly, rule-governed sequences of behaviour. Interactants usually synchronize their turns well and turn-taking, as we discussed in the last chapter, is generally very smooth. Habitually, only one person has the floor at any one time and violations of this turn-taking rule, when they do occur, have been found to be brief (Sacks *et al.* 1974; Beattie and Barnard 1979).

Interruption in conversation in part represents a major violation of the basic turn-taking rule. Most interruptions involve two speakers attempting to talk simultaneously and most studies define interruption on the basis of the occurrence of simultaneous speech (Jaffe and Feldstein 1970; Cook and Lalljee 1972; Rutter and Stephenson 1977), or on the basis of simultaneous turn-claimings (Duncan 1972, 1973) which excludes, for example, simultaneous speech resulting from overlaps involving listener attention signals or back-channels (Yngve 1970). Interruption would also, however, seem to occur when speakers lose the floor before they had intended to relinquish it, leaving their current utterance incomplete. This may occur when the auditor seizes the floor during an encoding pause (Goldman-Eisler 1968;

Beattie 1979a) in the floor-holder's speech. Ferguson (1976, 1977) has termed such interruptions 'silent interruptions'. Meltzer, Morris and Hayes (1971) have also recognized that such interruptions may occur — 'We are not concerned here with interruptions which do not involve simultaneous speech, for example, the well-timed contribution from another which diverts attention from the chain of the previous speaker's ideas to another topic' (Meltzer *et al.* 1971, p. 393). (This selective focus was defensible in their study because they were concerned only with the effects of vocal amplitude during simultaneous speech on the outcome of the interruption.)

A number of studies have demonstrated that interruption in conversation is affected by a number of social variables. Rim (1977) found that in three-person discussion groups, less intelligent people interrupted more frequently than the more intelligent people. He also found that individuals who were high in neuroticism interrupted more often than less neurotic individuals, and extroverts interrupted, and spoke simultaneously, more often than introverts. (One striking omission from this study, however, is that 'interruption' is not defined. All that we do know is that interruptions are not defined solely on the basis of the occurrence of simultaneous speech, as in many other studies, because the levels of interruption and simultaneous speech are not the same.) Feldstein, Alberti, Ben Debba and Welkowitz (1974) (cited by Feldstein and Welkowitz 1978) analysed the relationship between frequency of initiation of simultaneous speech and the personality characteristics of subjects (all female) as indexed by the Cattell 16PF. They found that 'Women who are relaxed, complacent, secure and not overly dependent on the approval of others tend to initiate more simultaneous speech than women who are generally apprehensive, self-reproaching, tense and frustrated' (Feldstein and Welkowitz 1978, p. 357). But in addition, Feldstein *et al.* found that the personality characteristics of their subjects' conversational partners also affected the rate of simultaneous speech, such that 'women tend to initiate more simultaneous speech when they converse with others who are cooperative, attentive, emotionally mature and talkative than with others who are aloof, critical, emotionally labile, introspective, silent and self-sufficient'. Similarly, Natale, Entin and Jaffe (1979) found that the personality characteristics both of subjects and of their conversational partners were related to rate of interruption. They found that frequency of interruption is inversely related to social anxiety (e.g. fear of negative evaluation) and to speech anxiety, but positively related to confidence as a speaker, i.e. more confident people interrupt more. They also found that 'the more confident the partner felt about speaking, the higher the proportion of successful interruptions by the other subject' (approximately 18% of the predicted variance was accounted for by the partner's speech confidence (Natale *et al.* 1979, p. 875)).

Zimmerman and West (1975) have, however, probably reported the most striking effects of social variables on interruption in conversation. They found that in male–female conversation men interrupt much more frequently than women. In fact, in ten male–female conversations, of a routine type, they found that virtually all the interruptions were initiated by men – the only instance recorded by Zimmerman and West of a female-initiated interruption occurred when a female teaching assistant interrupted a male undergraduate. Zimmerman and West note, however, that this same undergraduate had interrupted the female assistant eleven times to her two. Sex differences in frequency of interruption have also been reported by Esposito (1979) who found that boys (between 3.5 and 4.8 years old) interrupted girls more frequently than vice versa; and by Natale *et al.* in the study already mentioned. Zimmerman and West interpret their results in terms of male dominance and the power relationships between men and women: 'just as male dominance is exhibited through male control of macro-institutions in society, it is also exhibited through control of at least a part of one micro-institution' (Zimmerman and West 1975, p. 125). Interruption has traditionally been interpreted as a sign of dominance in the psychological literature (Farina 1960; Mishler and Waxler 1968; Hetherington, Stouwie and Ridberg 1971; Jacob 1974, 1975). But more recently some authors have cautiously suggested that it may not always reflect or signal dominance. For example, Gallois and Markel (1975) have provided evidence to suggest that interruptions may have different psychological relevance during different phases of a conversation, it may actually signal heightened involvement rather than dominance or discomfort (Long 1972). Meltzer *et al.* (1971) have emphasized that 'it would be a mistake . . . to infer that each interruption event is a miniature battle for ascendancy' (p. 392). Natale *et al.* (1979) found that a person who has a high need for social approval tends to interrupt more often, and that at least some interruptions may serve to express 'joint enthusiasm' (p. 875). Ferguson (1977) actually investigated the relationship between interruption and the dominance of interactants. She did not find any significant relationship between overall measures of interruption and dominance, contrary to the traditional view. She did, however, find that those subjects who used a lot of overlaps (which involve simultaneous speech but in which the original speaker's utterance appears complete) rated themselves as highly dominant. Zimmerman and West, in their study, had also investigated overlaps and found that men used these much more frequently than women. Overlaps, of course, demand a certain amount of skill on the part of interactants in that they involve the ability to predict possible completion points. This ability reflects a certain psycholinguistic competence.

Recent evidence suggests that the relationship between interruptions and dominance is much more complex than had previously been assumed. Interruptions are a social phenomenon affected by many variables including the personality characteristics of subjects as well as the personality characteristics of their fellow interactants. It has also now been suggested that interruption may be indicative of social relationships other than those purely of dominance. Nevertheless, the striking sex difference reported by Zimmerman and West is clearly in need of further investigation. Zimmerman and West studied only a specific set of social contexts – most of their conversations were recorded in public places in a university and some in private residences where everyday 'chit-chat' takes place, and they themselves question the generality of their results (see also Beattie 1982a). They do not claim that male–female conversations will invariably exhibit the asymmetric patterns they observed, and they suggest that 'A challenging task for further research is the specification of conditions under which . . . sex roles become relevant to the conduct of conversationalists' (p. 125). The following study explores the relationship between sex of interactant and interruption in a different type of natural conversation – university tutorials – and in addition, the study investigates the relationship between formal status within the group and interruptions.

Interruptions, sex and status

PROCEDURE

Analyses presented below were based on data drawn from videotapes of ten tutorial groups held at the University of Sheffield (from Beattie 1981c). All participants had given permission to be video-recorded. Five of the tutorial groups involved male tutors, five involved female tutors. All tutorials held by male tutors consisted of both male and female students, but three of the five female tutors supervised an all-female group (these were tutorial groups 6, 9 and 10). Half of the groups were first years, and half second years. In each group there were from three to six students plus a tutor. Status is held to be associated with position in the group – tutor versus undergraduate student. The groups were arranged in incomplete circles, with a table in front of the one-way mirror in the observation room in which the filming occurred, to prevent any members of the group turning their back to the camera. The video-recording was done behind the one-way mirror using a Sony AV-362OCE solid-state video-recorder, and an ITC Link camera, and a wide-angle lens. A microphone was suspended in the room, which allowed all utterances to be clearly recorded. There was considerable variability in the actual length of the tutorial, the shortest being 29 minutes, the longest being 60 minutes. The total length of conversation analysed was 491 minutes. The videotapes were played back on a Sanyo Video Edit machine. The time of each speaker-switch was noted, and a modified version of the categorization scheme devised by Ferguson (1977) was employed (see Figure 6.1). Inter-observer reliability between two judges in applying this categorization scheme was 88%, Kappa = 0.85 (Cohen 1960; Leach 1979). The test–retest reliability was 96%. Reliability was calculated on the basis of a sample of 50 speaker-switches, 10 of each category.

Figure 6.1 Classification of interruptions and smooth speaker-switches

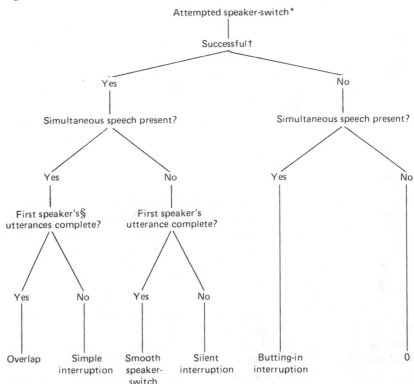

* Brief interjectory remarks (such as yeah, mm-hmm, exactly, etc.) are not treated as instances of speaker-switching (following Ferguson, 1977). These interjections correspond to Yngve's (1970) 'back-channel behaviours'. Dittmann and Llewellyn's (1967) 'listener responses' and Kendon's (1967) 'accompaniment signals'. Their function seems to be the very opposite of effecting a change in speaker (see Duncan, 1972; Ferguson, 1977).

† By 'successful' it is meant that the initiator of the 'attempted interruption' takes the floor. In a butting-in interruption − an unsuccessful attempted interruption − the interruptor stops before gaining control of the floor.

§ 'Completeness' was judged intuitively on the basis of intonational, syntactic and semantic features in the verbal channel as well as by analysis of nonverbal behaviour. Gestures can and do substitute for speech. In one case a tutor ended his turn with 'so you might imagine it would be . . .' and gestured down. This would have been categorized as an interruption if only an audio-recording had been available because it was syntactically and intonationally incomplete. However, on the basis of the analysis of the videotape the iconic gesture which substituted for 'down' was noted and it was categorized as a smooth speaker-switch − utterance complete with no simultaneous speech. The classification of 'completeness' was done at the point where the first speaker stopped vocalizing and this judgment was not dependent on the point at which the second speaker started vocalizing.

1. *Smooth speaker-switch*
Example:
Tutor: But i-i-i-it's important within / within the confines of the figure
              (300)
Student$_1$:   Within the confines of the figure yes, but not / in the general
              visual field . . .

2. *Simple interruption*
Example:
Tutor: . . . so he / he gives the impression that he he wasn't able to train
              them up. { *Now*
Student$_1$:   { *He* didn't try
              hard enough heh heh heh.

3. *Overlap*
Example:
Student$_2$:   . . . it doesn't matter where it is, if it's on the edge / near near
              the edge of your periphery / or you know right at the centre
              because you can move your head / and it'll move you know
              { *it'll move with it*
Tutor: { *Yes, I* don't
              I don't think we're disagreeing about that, because I think /
              what I interpreted this to mean . . .

4. *Butting-in interruption*
Example:
Student$_2$:   . . . and you know he said that's rubbish / that seems to go back
              to
Tutor: { *well*   }
Student$_2$:   that really { *because* } I mean why does he say . . . and the right
              side was on the left and / you / know
Tutor: { *oh oh you you still you still* }

Student₂: $\left\{$ *and you still keep* $\right\}$ that sort of order you know so I / will
                 you know

5.   *Silent interruption*
Example:
Student₂: Yeah I thought you meant its position with respect to everything
            else not the actual
                          (200)
Student₁: You know wherever you've got / the parts I mean approxi-
            mately in the right positions . . .

Symbols used in transcription are as follows (adapted from Schegloff and
Sacks 1973):
/   indicates unfilled pause ≥ 200 milliseconds
(x) indicates switching pause of x milliseconds
{   with italics indicates simultaneous speech

RESULTS

Table 6.1 shows the relative frequency of smooth speaker-switches
and interruptions within the ten tutorial groups. The percentage of
speaker-switches involving some form of interruption ranged between
23.5% and 40.4% with a mean of 34.3%. The three all-female tutorial
groups (6, 9 and 10) did not differ significantly from the other seven
mixed-sex groups in terms of the percentage of speaker-swithces
involving interruption (Mann–Whitney U test, $U = 9$, $n_1 = 3$,
$n_2 = 7$, n.s.; 2-tailed test).

Table 6.1 Relative frequency of smooth speaker-switches and interruptions
in tutorial groups

Tutorial group	All speaker-switches	Smooth speaker-switches	Interruptions	Percentage interruptions
1	128	92	36	28.1
2	168	104	64	38.1
3	304	204	100	32.9
4	270	164	106	39.3
5	151	90	61	40.4
6	117	73	44	37.6
7	115	88	27	23.5
8	199	137	62	31.2
9	86	57	29	33.7
10	84	56	28	33.3
TOTAL	1,622	1,065	557	Mean = 34.3

Table 6.2 Relative frequency of smooth speaker-switches and interruptions when students take the floor from tutors (tutor–students), tutors take the floor from students (student–tutor) and students from students

		Tutor–student			Student–tutor		
Tutorial group	Smooth speaker-switches	Interruptions	Percentage interruption	Smooth speaker-switches	Interruptions	Percentage interruption
1	41	18	30.5	46	14	23.3
2	38	26	40.6	46	17	27.0
3	85	34	28.6	95	21	18.1
4	66	50	43.1	81	33	29.0
5	42	23	35.4	39	29	42.7
6	34	23	40.4	38	18	32.1
7	39	8	17.0	40	9	18.4
8	42	37	46.8	65	14	17.7
9	20	19	48.7	30	9	23.1
10	26	15	36.6	27	10	27.6
TOTAL	433	253	Mean = 36.9	507	174	Mean = 25.8

		Student–student	
1	5	4	44.4
2	20	21	51.2
3	24	45	65.2
4	17	23	57.5
5	9	9	50.0
6	1	3	75.0
7	9	10	52.6
8	30	11	26.8
9	7	1	14.3
10	3	3	50.0
TOTAL	125	130	Mean = 51.0

Table 6.2 shows the relative frequency of smooth speaker-switches and interruptions when tutors lose the floor to students, students lose the floor to tutors, and students lose the floor to students. (Interruptions where more than one auditor began speaking at exactly the same moment, which were relatively rare, are not discussed in this paper.) A mean of 36.9% of all speaker-switches involve some form of interruption when students take the floor from tutors, but 25.8% when tutors take the floor from students. However 51.0% of all speaker-switches involve some form of interruption when students take the floor from other students. The percentage of switches involving interruption was compared firstly for tutor–student switches and student–tutor switches and this proved to be significant (Wilcoxon matched-pairs signed-ranks test, $T = 4$, $n = 10$, $p < 0.02$; 2-tailed

test). In other words, students interrupt tutors significantly more often than vice versa. Students also interrupt other students significantly more often than tutors interrupt students (Wilcoxon test, $T = 2$, $n = 10$, $p < 0.01$; 2-tailed test). Students do not, however, interrupt students significantly more often than they interrupt tutors (Wilcoxon test, $T = 13$, $n = 10$, $\therefore$ n.s.; 2-tail).

Table 6.3 shows the relative frequency of smooth speaker-switches and interruptions when males take the floor from females, males from other males, females from males and females from other females. 33.8% of all speaker-switches involve some form of interruption when females take the floor from males and 34.1% when males take the floor from females. This difference was not, however, significant (Wilcoxon test, $T = 13$, $= 7$, $\therefore$ n.s.; 2-tail). Also males do not interrupt

Table 6.3 Relative frequency of smooth speaker-switches and interruptions when females take the floor from males (male—female), males take the floor from females (female—male), males from males, and females from females

Tutorial group	Male—female			Female—male		
	Smooth speaker-switches	Interruptions	Percentage interruptions	Smooth speaker-switches	Interruptions	Percentage interruptions
1	19	10	34.5	25	3	10.7
2	39	24	38.1	44	20	31.3
3	52	40	43.5	57	31	35.2
4	25	11	30.6	19	17	47.2
5	32	20	38.5	31	23	42.6
6	φ	φ	φ	φ	φ	φ
7	27	10	27.0	27	8	22.9
8	52	17	24.6	36	34	48.6
9	φ	φ	φ	φ	φ	φ
10	φ	φ	φ	φ	φ	φ
TOTAL	246	132	Mean = 33.8	239	136	Mean = 34.1

	Male—male			Female—female		
1	46	21	31.3	2	2	50.0
2	15	12	44.4	6	8	57.1
3	90	16	15.1	5	13	72.2
4	120	78	39.4	0	0	0
5	24	11	39.4	3	7	70.0
6	φ	φ	φ	73	44	37.6
7	0	0	0	34	9	20.9
8	7	2	22.2	42	9	17.6
9	φ	φ	φ	57	29	33.7
10	φ	φ	φ	56	28	33.3
	302	140	Mean = 31.7	278	149	Mean = 34.9

females significantly more frequently than they do other males (Wilcoxon test, $T = 8$, $n = 7$, $\therefore$ n.s.; 2-tail), nor do males and females differ in the frequency with which they interrupt males (Wilcoxon test, $T = 8$, $n = 7$, $\therefore$ n.s.; 2-tail). Females do not interrupt females significantly more frequently than they interrupt males (Wilcoxon test, $T = 9$, $n = 7$, $\therefore$ n.s.; 2-tail and Mann–Whitney U test $n_1 = 3$, $n_2 = 7$, $U = 10$, $\therefore$ n.s.; 2-tail combined probability n.s.). Females and males do not differ significantly in the frequency with which they interrupt females (Wilcoxon test, $T = 12$, $n = 7$, $\therefore$ n.s.; 2-tail, and Mann–Whitney U test, $n_1 = 3$, $n_2 = 7$, $U = 10$, $\therefore$ n.s.; 2-tail combined probability n.s.).

Interactions between sex and status

Table 6.4 (a and b) shows the various interactions between sex and status in interruption and the non-parametric analyses used to test the effects of different combinations of these variables on interruptions. As can be seen from Table 6.4 all of the effects proved non-significant. However, some striking effects did emerge. When students take the floor from other students, almost half the speaker-switches involve some form of interruption (in the case of female students taking the floor from male students the mean percentage is 53.2, and 47.7 for male students taking the floor from female students). However, there was no significant difference when the proportion of floor-switches involving interruption was compared for male or female students taking the floor either from other students or tutors of the same sex (see Table 6.4).

Table 6.5 shows the relative frequencies of the four different types of interruption identified by Ferguson (1977). Overlaps are the commonest form of interruption, being more than four times as common as silent interruption, the least common kind. Nevertheless, almost 10% of all interruptions are silent interruptions (i.e. interrup-

Table 6.4a Mean percentage of interruptions, by sex and status of interrupter and person interrupted

			Interrupter			
			Tutor		Student	
			Male	Female	Male	Female
Initial	Tutor	Male	ϕ^a	ϕ^b	36.8[c]	34.7[d]
speaker		Female	ϕ^e	ϕ^f	43.5[g]	36.6[h]
(i.e. person	Student	Male	25.8[i]	18.3[j]	42.9[k]	53.2[l]
interrupted)		Female	28.4[m]	25.3[n]	47.7[o]	54.9[p]

Table 6.4b Non-parametric tests comparing percentage of interruption by sex and status of interrupter and person interrupted

Type of Comparison	Cells Compared	Non-parametric Test	Results	Significance Level
Sex of interrupter (holding status constant)	c vs. d	Wilcoxon	T=6 (n=6)	n.s.
	g vs. h	χ^2	$\chi^2=1.172$	n.s.
	i vs j	χ^2	$\chi^2=1.877$	n.s.
	k vs. l	Wilcoxon	T=3 (n=7)	n.s.
	m vs. n	Mann–Whitney	U=12 ($n_1=5$; $n_2=5$)	n.s.
	o vs. p	Wilcoxon and Mann–Whitney	T=8 (n=7)	n.s.
			U=9 ($n_1=3$; $n_2=7$)	
Sex of person interrupted (holding status constant)	c vs. g	χ^2	$\chi^2=1.182$	n.s.
	d vs. h	Mann–Whitney	U=11 ($n_1=5$; $n_2=5$)	n.s.
	i vs. m	Wilcoxon	T=5 (n=5)	n.s.
	j vs. n	χ^2	$\chi^2=1.527$	n.s.
	k vs. o	Wilcoxon	T=3 (n=7)	n.s.
	l vs. p	Wilcoxon and Mann–Whitney	T=13 (n=7)	n.s.
			U=13 ($n_1=3$; $\dot{n}_2=7$)	
Sex. reversing roles	l vs. o	Wilcoxon	T=8 (n=7)	n.s.
Status of interrupter (holding sex constant)	i vs. k	Wilcoxon and Mann–Whitney	T=5, U=1	n.s.
	j vs. l	Wilcoxon and Mann–Whitney	T=0, U=0	n.s.
	m vs. o	Wilcoxon and Mann–Whitney	T=5, U=4	n.s.
	n vs. p	Wilcoxon and Mann–Whitney	T=4, U=5	n.s.
Status of person interrupted (holding sex constant)	c vs. k	Wilcoxon and Mann–Whitney	T=2 (n=5), U=1 ($n_1=2$); $n_2=5$)	n.s.
	d vs. l	Mann–Whitney	U=9 ($n_1=5$; $n_2=7$)	n.s.
	g vs. o	χ^2	$\chi^2=0.305$	n.s.
	h vs. p	Wilcoxon and Mann–Whitney	T=6 (n=5), U=5 ($n_1=5$; $n_2=10$)	n.s.

Table 6.5 Relative frequency of different categories of interruption

Tutorial group	Simple interruption	Category of interruption Overlap	Butting-in interruption	Silent interruption
1	7	17	7	5
2	15	27	14	8
3	31	43	16	10
4	39	51	10	6
5	19	28	7	7
6	13	14	13	4
7	9	11	2	5
8	26	24	7	5
9	13	11	2	3
10	11	10	6	1
TOTAL	183	236	84	54
Percentages of total number of interruptions	32.9	42.4	15.1	9.7

tions which do not involve any simultaneous speech). Overlaps are significantly more common than either butting-in interruptions or silent interruptions (in both cases Wilcoxon matched-pairs signed-ranks test, $T = 0$, $n = 10$, $p < 0.01$; 2-tailed test) but not significantly more common than simple interruptions (Wilcoxon test, $T = 9\frac{1}{2}$, $n = 10$, $\therefore$ n.s.; 2-tailed test).

Table 6.6 shows the relative frequencies of each of these types of interruption when a target person of either sex is interrupted either by a male or a female — in none of the four categories of interruption was there any significant difference between males and females. A Wilcoxon test and Mann–Whitney U test showed that for simple interruptions, $T = 13$ ($n = 7$), $U = 6$ ($n_1 = 3$, $n_2 = 7$) $\therefore$ combined probability n.s. For each of the other three comparisons the T and U values are included (*n*s are the same as for simple interruptions). For overlaps $T = 8$, $U = 4$; for butting-in interruptions $T = 10\frac{1}{2}$, $U = 8$; and for silent interruptions $T = 9$, $U = 9$. Therefore, sex of interactant did not have any significant effect on the frequency of any category of interruption shown in non-dyadic interaction.

Table 6.6 Relative frequency of each category of interruption as related to sex (expressed as a percentage of the total number of interruptions in that group)

Tutorial group	Simple interruption		Overlap	
	Person–Male	Person–Female	Person–Male	Person–Female
1	16.7	25.0	45.8	50.0
2	21.9	25.0	37.5	46.9
3	34.0	28.3	44.7	41.5
4	35.8	45.5	47.4	54.6
5	35.3	25.9	41.2	51.9
6	φ	29.6	φ	31.8
7	12.5	42.1	62.5	31.6
8	52.8	26.9	30.6	50.0
9	φ	44.8	φ	37.9
10	φ	39.3	φ	35.7
Means	29.9	33.2	44.2	43.2
Ns	93	90	119	117

Tutorial group	Butting-in interruption		Silent interruption	
	Person–Male	Person–Female	Person–Male	Person–Female
1	20.8	16.7	16.7	8.3
2	31.3	12.5	9.4	15.6
3	12.8	18.9	8.5	11.3
4	10.5	φ	6.3	φ
5	14.7	7.4	8.8	14.8
6	φ	29.6	φ	9.1
7	φ	10.5	25.0	15.8
8	8.3	15.4	8.3	7.7
9	φ	6.9	φ	10.3
10	φ	21.4	φ	3.6
Means	14.1	13.9	11.9	9.7
Ns	39	45	25	29

The effects of status on category of interruption used was then analysed (see Table 6.7).

Table 6.7 Relative frequency of each category of interruptions as relation to status (expressed as a percentage of the total number of interruptions within that group)

Tutorial group	Simple interruption		Overlap	
	Person–Tutor	Person–Student	Person–Tutor	Person–Student
1	21.4	18.2	50.0	45.5
2	29.4	21.3	47.1	40.4
3	23.8	32.9	52.4	40.5
4	18.2	45.2	66.7	39.7
5	27.6	34.4	44.8	46.9
6	22.2	34.6	38.9	26.9
7	22.2	38.9	55.6	33.3
8	35.7	43.8	50.0	35.4
9	11.1	60.0	66.7	25.0
10	40.0	38.9	50.0	27.8
Means	25.2	36.8	52.2	36.1
Ns	43	140	91	145

Tutorial group	Butting-in interruptions		Silent interruption	
	Person–Tutor	Person–Student	Person–Tutor	Person–student
1	28.6	13.6	0	22.7
2	23.5	21.3	0	17.0
3	4.8	19.0	19.1	7.6
4	9.1	9.6	6.1	5.5
5	17.2	6.3	10.3	12.5
6	33.3	26.9	5.6	11.5
7	11.1	5.6	11.1	22.2
8	14.3	10.4	0	10.4
9	11.1	5.0	11.1	10.0
10	10.0	27.8	0	5.6
Means	16.3	14.6	6.3	12.5
Ns	28	56	12	42

Here it was found that the relative frequency of simple interruptions and overlaps were affected by status within the group. Simple interruptions were more frequently used by students than by tutors (Wilcoxon test, $T = 8$, $n = 10$, $p < 0.05$; 2-tail). Overlaps, on the other hand, were significantly more frequently used by tutors than by students (Wilcoxon test, $T = 1$, $n = 10$, $p < 0.01$; 2-tail). Status within the tutorial group did not significantly affect either the proportion of butting-in interruptions (Wilcoxon test, $T = 19$, $n = 10$, $\therefore$ n.s.; 2-tail) or silent interruptions (Wilcoxon test, $T = 11$, $n = 10$, $\therefore$ n.s.; 2-tail).

DISCUSSION

This study explored the nature and origin of interruption in non-dyadic conversations – a sample of university tutorials were video-recorded and analysed. Interruption was found to be a common and prominent feature of the turn-taking system accounting for over one-third of all speaker-switches (see Table 6.1). It appears to be much more common in non-dyadic than dyadic conversations – Beattie and Barnard (1979) report that only 10.6% of speaker-switches involved interruption in a series of dyadic university tutorials (but it should be noted that a more restricted definition of interruption was employed in the earlier study which excluded the category of silent interruptions analysed in the present study). If we exclude the category of silent interruptions in the present study to make the two studies exactly comparable, the percentage of interruptions in the present study is still 31.0% – considerably higher than the 10.6% reported by Beattie and Barnard (1979). This suggests that in non-dyadic conversations, interactants tend to gain control of the floor more often by interrupting than in dyadic conversations. This, of course, makes sense because in non-dyadic groups there are more listeners to whom the current speaker can potentially hand over the floor. This discrepancy in rate of interruption between dyadic and non-dyadic conversation perhaps highlights the danger in drawing general conclusions about conversational interaction on the basis of micro-analysis of dyadic conversations alone. However, it is interesting to note that the same rank ordering (in terms of frequency) of categories of interruption was found in this study as in a study of dyadic conversation which applied the same basic classificatory scheme (see Ferguson 1977, p. 298). Overlaps were the most common category of interruption in both studies followed by simple interruptions and butting-in interruptions with silent interruptions the least common (see Table 6.5). Most common forms of interruption seem to involve some simultaneous speech.

This study, in contrast to that of Zimmerman and West (1975), found no sex differences in either the frequency or type of interruption. In the present study males interrupted females 34.1% of the time, and females interrupted males 33.8% of the time (see Table 6.3). Zimmerman and West had found that virtually all interruptions and all overlaps, without exception, in male–female conversations were produced by males. On methodological grounds it should be noted that there are important differences in the definition of interruption in the Zimmerman and West study as compared with the present study. Zimmerman and West's concept of interruption corresponds most closely with the category 'simple interruption' in the present study. Their concept of 'overlap' would, however, seem to correspond reasonably closely with this concept as used in this study. However, neither of these two more specific categories distinguished male and female interactants in the present study (see Table 6.6). In interrupting, males used overlaps on average 44.2% of the time compared with 43.2% for females. Males used simple interruption on average 29.9% of the time compared with 33.2% for females. What is interesting to note is that the reason sex differences did not emerge in this study is not because males were interrupting less than in previous studies but because women were interrupting more. This was especially true in the case of female students who tended to interrupt men more frequently than female tutors did (although this trend failed to reach significance). Female students' interruption of male students was very high – accounting for more than half the speaker-switches from male students to female students.

One may speculate that sex differences in conversational behaviour of the type observed by Zimmerman and West (1975) may be limited to those types of conversation in which women are not deliberately trying to make an impression – this presumably would be especially true in many dyadic male–female conversations where there is not a third party observing the proceedings. However, when the social context demands that interactants make a good impression (for example, in tutorials), women can and do use interruption as frequently as men.

Sex differences had no significant effect on either the amount or type of interruption in tutorial discussions. Status within the group, however, had a very significant effect. Firstly, it was found that students interrupted tutors significantly more often than tutors interrupted students. The mean percentage of speaker-switches involving interruption when students take the floor from tutors was 36.9 compared with 25.8 when tutors take the floor from students (see Table 6.2). This would not have been predicted from any hypothesis that holds that interruption is invariably a reflection of dominance in social interaction, because presumably tutors would normally be identified as the dominant members of tutorial groups. But there was an even more striking effect obtained in this study which may hold a clue to the significance and meaning of interruption in this context. Students interrupted other students significantly more frequently than tutors interrupted students – indeed, about twice as often. These results make a good deal of sense if one thinks about the dynamics of tutorial groups. In the English university system a student's performance in tutorials may be taken into account in his overall academic assessment. There is, therefore, some pressure on students to make a good impression in tutorials by making some contribution to the discussion. However, in non-dyadic tutorial groups, when a student talks he almost invariably addresses himself (in terms of orientation, gaze, etc.) to the tutor rather than to another student. Even when a student is strongly disagreeing with another student, he often still addresses the tutor, presumably for the tutor to act as mediator. (I have not quantified these observations but this picture clearly emerges from study of the video-recorded tutorials.) If one students wishes to speak while another has the floor, then it makes sense for him to attempt to obtain the floor by interrupting, because if he waits, the floor will be handed over to the tutor. (Undoubtedly, non-verbal behaviours like gaze will be implicated in this process. Gaze is probably a more effective signals for handing over the floor in non-dyadic (Weisbrod 1965), than in dyadic conversations, where its significance is still somewhat unclear (Kendon 1967; Duncan 1972; Beattie 1978a, 1979b).) When the tutor is talking, he often directs his speech largely at one individual. Again, if a student other than the direct addressee wishes to take the floor, it makes sense to obtain it by interrupting. Tutors, on the other hand, probably interrupt less than students because there is an onus on them to encourage students to talk. It should be remembered, however, that tutors still interrupt students in 25.8% of all speaker-switches which casts a different light on the behaviour of tutors in tutorial groups than might be obtained from self-reports of tutors. Tutors often bemoan the frequency of their contributions to tutorials and suggest that they only repeatedly take the floor because no one else is prepared to. However, tutors often, in fact, do not permit students in the groups to formulate a reply to any expressed opinion because they insert their own contribution just before the end of a turn is reach, i.e. by overlapping. The students in these tutorial groups, on the other hand, used simple interruptions more frequently than tutors. These are interruptions where the current speaker had not reached a possible completion point

— students are therefore cutting across in the middle of a turn. These observations suggest that because of the demands of the situation, tutors are attempting to encourage students to speak by interrupting at least less frequently than students, and, when they do interrupt, they tend to overlap rather than cut across in the middle of a student's turn. Students, on the other hand, because of the primary structure of tutorial groups, with the tutor as perceptual centre, seem forced to cut in on tutor's and other students' speech in order to make some contribution to the discussion.

This study would seem to have important implications for research in conversational interaction. In line with Ferguson's (1977) study, it suggests that interruption is not a unitary phenomenon. Different categories of interruption are affected by different variables, and only some seem to be related to variables which might be thought to reflect dominance (however defined). The use in many previous studies of an undifferentiated concept of interruption as a measure of 'dominance' (as discussed in the Introduction to this chapter) would seem to be highly questionable. The study also suggests that social context will have an important effect on some of the most basic processes of conversation. Sex differences in the violation of the turn-taking system are not a universal feature of conversation — women certainly seem to possess the interactional competence to engage in interruption as frequently and as effectively as men, when required.

Interruptions in political interviews

The previous study (Beattie 1981c) involved the analysis of turn-taking in groups, here we switch again to dyads but dyads of a particular kind — political interviews. Who interrupts whom in these interviews and why? What mechanisms mediate interruption in televised political interviews?

This study presents some analyses of the speech and conversational styles of two of Britain's leading political figures — Mrs Margaret Thatcher, a Conservative who is now Prime Minister, and Mr James Callaghan, a Labour politician who was formerly Prime Minister. The corpus on which the analysis is based consists of two televised interviews shown on British television in April 1979, just before the 1979 general election. They were shown on ITV's *TV Eye* programme. At the time of the initial recording, the political role of the two politicians was different. Mr Callaghan was then Prime Minister; Mrs Thatcher was leader of the Opposition.

The analysis presented in this paper again focusses on conversational turn-taking in these interviews and the study considers other aspects of speech only where they are thought to be relevant to turn-taking.

In social psychology, as we have already discussed, the majority of research has attempted to link aspects of turn-taking and interruption to fairly gross social variables such as sex, intelligence, degree of extraversion, etc. This study differs in that it considers the turn-taking style of individual speakers. Such an enterprise may prove interesting on at least two accounts. First, we may learn something about the variability of a central aspect of conversational behaviour as displayed by two very different individuals placed in a similar situation. Second, we may at least speculate how any observed behavioural differences may influence other people's perceptions of these politicians. There is no doubt, of course, that nonsemantic aspects of speech in conversation do have a strong influence on interpersonal perception. A number of studies have even suggested that the nonverbal channel in communication has a greater effect on the communication of interpersonal attitudes than the verbal channel (Argyle *et al.* 1970; Argyle *et al.* 1971), but see Chapter 1. There is also evidence that people will ascribe certain traits to individuals on the basis of particular aspects of their nonverbal and conversational behaviour. Lay and Burton (1968) found that people ascribe desirable traits to fluent speakers and undesirable traits to hesitant speakers who used frequent pauses and repetitions. Cook and Smith (1972) found that individuals who averted eye-gaze in interaction were perceived as 'nervous' and 'lacking in confidence'. Kleck and Nuessle (1968) found that people who displayed little eye-gaze in interaction were perceived as 'defensive' and 'evasive'. More recently, research has shown that in real-life situations, aspects of conversational style critically affect interpersonal judgement, such that success or failure in selection interviews depends upon behaviours such as amount of eye contact, smiling, and head movement (Forbes and Jackson 1980). Given the centrality of the turn-taking mechanism, individual differences in the style of its operation will undoubtedly influence interpersonal perception. Therefore, turn-taking in political interviews will be especially important since, for politicians, interpersonal perception is of crucial significance.

The emergence of the televised political interview as the chief vehicle for getting a political message across makes skills of dialogue (including turn-taking skills) all the more important. 'Intimate' conversations between a politician and an interviewer are broadcast to millions of viewers who witness at close quarters the speech and nonverbal style of the politician. Many people seem to have become aware of this, and before the last two general elections in Britain there was a good deal of consternation among British politicians that viewers were more likely to forget the content of the political message than the way it was delivered. Clearly, the modern politician must be as adept at the skills of dialogue as politicians from earlier generations were at the skills of oratory. Moreover, viewers are unlikely to excuse temporary lapses in performance, or to attribute deviations from perfect performance to the stresses and strains of the interview. There is considerable evidence to suggest that observers (as opposed to the actors themselves) are prone to explain behaviour in terms of the traits or personality of the individual concerned rather than in terms of the demands of the situation (see Ross 1977; Ross *et al.* 1977; Beattie 1979c). Any behaviours that appear discrepant in interviews will be used to infer personality traits and these inferences are likely to endure. Thus, any differences in turn-taking style may critically influence the viewers' perceptions of the politicians and may indeed lead to strong beliefs about the characters and personalities of the politicians concerned. Consequently, exploration of individual differences in turn-taking style becomes interesting and significant for reasons other than those of simply learning more about the phenomena in question.

In this study the turn-taking styles of Margaret Thatcher and Jim Callaghan are analysed and contrasted. Special attention is devoted to the frequency, nature, and significance of the interruptions that punctuate these interviews.

PROCEDURE

The analyses presented below were based on data drawn from videotapes of two televised interviews broadcast in April 1979. The interviews involved James Callaghan, interviewed by Llew Gardner, and Margaret Thatcher, interviewed by Denis Tuohy. Each interview lasted 25 minutes. The two interviews were recorded in different locations – Mr Callaghan was interviewed in 10 Downing Street, the official residence of the Prime Minister. Mrs Thatcher was interviewed in a television studio. These televised interviews were video-recorded by the author using a Sony VTR and a timer was mixed onto the recording, allowing identification of individual frames on the videotape.

The videotapes were played back and analysed on a Sanyo video edit machine. The time of each speaker-switch was noted and the accompanying speech was transcribed in considerable detail. Notes were also made on the transcripts of relevant nonverbal behaviour. A pause–phonation analysis using the pauseometer was also performed on selected speaker-turns of the two politicians from the beginning, middle, and end of the interviews, in order to calculate speech rate and articulation rate. Speech rate is defined as the number of words per minute of the whole utterance. Articulation rate is defined as a number of words per minute of the time spent in vocal activity (see Goldman-Eisler 1968, p. 24). The same equipment was also used to analyse switching-pauses (the period of joint silence bounded by the turns of different speakers), which are marked, where appropriate, on the examples provided.

Smooth speaker-switches and interruptions were again classified according to a categorization scheme devised by Ferguson (1977). Test–retest reliability in applying this categorization scheme was 93%. A better measure of reliability that takes into account 'chance agreement' is Cohen's Kappa (Cohen 1960). Kappa in this particular case was 0.89, indicating very high test–retest reliability.

Examples
  (1)   Smooth speaker-switch: exchange of turns, no simultaneous speech present, first speaker's utterance appears complete.

Example A
   MT: . . . I hope it will succeed / We can put the ball at / people's feet / Some of them will kick it.
      (0)
   DT: What about the people below the top rate tax payers. The people who you feel might come back to the country.

Example B
   JC: . . . the Conservative Attorney General / had to find this man called the official solicitor / in order to invent some piece of law to get them out again / Now for heaven's sake we've tried it and failed / Now we've got to go the other way.
      (200)
   LG: Mr. Callaghan / if polls are to be believed your own appeal.

  (2)   Simple interruption: exchange of turns, simultaneous speech present, first speaker's turn appears incomplete.

Example A
   JC: . . . and I don't claim to be infallible. You may remember in one of my ⎰ *earliest broad*−
   LG: ⎱ *a degree*
      of fallibility Prime Minister.

Example B
MT: . . . People forget / that he was one of the best
     ministers of social / services this country's ever had
     { *and he*
DT: { *but that's* one kind of public spending.

(3) Overlap: exchange of turns, simultaneous speech present, first
    speaker's turn *reaches* completion. In example C the
    interruption extends for more than a sentence (7 words in all),
    but the first speaker nevertheless manages to complete his
    utterance; thus the speaker-switch is classified as an overlap.

Example A
MT: . . . it cannot tell you exactly what economies it's going
     to make in each department { *it just can't*
DT: { *can it tell you*
     that it will be able to make any?

    Example B
LG: . . . I wonder whether people feel that this is because
     the Labour Party has run out of some steam. It hasn't
     so many { *new ideas*
JC: { *I think i- /*
     I think it's because they are / ah answers to what
     are / gross overclaims by the Conservative
     Party / . . .

    Example C
LG: Not every other other country ev-every other mal-
     practice our driving / our driving the way we behave in
     the street /
     { *everything else why are trade unions different*
JC: { *look trade unions are a voluntary body*
     trade unions are covered by the law too / they are
     covered by the law in a great many ways.

(4) Butting-in interruption: no exchange of turns, simultaneous
    speech present.

Example A
JC: . . . but if anybody suggests that in a democracy you
     can do more than that / then they're saying this
     shouldn't be a
     { *democracy*   }
LG: { *everybody else's malpractices* }

JC: { *now heavens* {
         for heaven's sake / in Eastern Europe / you can / you
         can / perhaps enforce guidelines.

Example B

MT: . . . if you've got the money in your pocket / you can
         choose / whether you spend it on things which attract
         Value Added Tax / or not /
DT: { *You s—*
MT: { *and*   the main necessities don't
DT: You say a little on Value Added Tax

(5) Silent interruption: exchange of turns, no simultaneous
     speech, first speaker's utterance appears incomplete.

Example A

DT: . . . and you gave a list which included / most of the
         public sector workers who have been on strike in the
         last few months / you said you would / pursue those
         disruptive elements with
                        (0)
MT: unremitting hostility { *quite right*
DT: { *yes and is that a word*
MT: you have seen destructive elements today / yesterday
         on the television

This example may seem ambiguous in terms of classification, since
   floor-holders often hand over the floor in conversation by
   allowing a listener to complete their utterance. It can be
   argued, however, that the above example is not a smooth
   speaker-switch with the end intentionally omitted. The
   grounds for its classification as a silent interruption depend
   crucially on the intonation of the turn and the subsequent
   behavior of DT, in that DT immediately attempts to regain
   the floor. It should be noted that DT's attempt to regain the
   floor is unsuccessful (resulting in a butting-in interruption).

RESULTS

In the Callaghan interview, Callaghan held the floor 38 times, and
Gardner, who put the first question and contributed the last turn, held
the floor 39 times. There were thus 76 exchanges of turn. In addition,
there were 8 butting-in interruptions, i.e. interruptions in which there
was no exchange of turn. In all there were 84 smooth speaker-switches
and interruptions in this interview.

In the Thatcher interview, Thatcher held the floor 26 times and Tuohy 26 times. There were thus 51 exchanges of turn. This means that the average length of turn was longer in this interview than in the Callaghan interview, because both interviews lasted exactly 25 minutes. There were 11 butting-in interruptions in this interview and therefore there were 62 smooth speaker-switches and interruptions in all in the interview.

Table 6.8 Relative frequency of smooth speaker-switches and interruptions in televised political interviews

Speaker$_1$ — Speaker$_2$	Smooth speaker-switch	Interruption
Margaret Thatcher — Denis Tuohy	17	19
Denis Tuohy — Margaret Thatcher	16	10
Jim Callaghan — Llew Gardner	28	14
Llew Gardner — Jim Callaghan	19	23
	80	66

Table 6.8 shows the relative frequency of smooth speaker-switches and interruptions in the two interviews. Interruptions account for 37.0% of all exchanges of turn and 45.2% of all attempted exchanges of turn. This compares with 10.6% for dyadic university tutorials and 6.3% for telephone conversations (Beattie and Barnard 1979). Clearly, interruptions are very common in political interviews. An interesting contrast between the two politicians is also immediately apparent — in the Thatcher interview the interviewer interrupts Margaret Thatcher almost twice as often as she interrupts him, whereas in the Callaghan interview, Jim Callaghan interrupts his interviewer more than the interviewer interrupts him. Margaret Thatcher is in fact interrupted significantly more frequently in her interview than Callaghan is in his ($x^2 = 3.05$, d.f. $= 1$, $p \simeq 0.05$).

The two politicians did not, however, differ significantly in the frequency with which they interrupted their interviews ($x^2 = 1.69$, d.f. $= 1$, n.s.). The percentage figures allow some interesting comparisons. Tuohy interrupted Thatcher 52.8% of the time and Callaghan interrupted Gardner 54.8% of the time. Thatcher interrupted Tuohy 38.5% of the time and Gardner interrupted Callaghan 33.3% of the time. Thus, in this respect, Tuohy was

behaving more like Jim Callaghan than Callaghan's interviewer
Gardner, and Margaret Thatcher was behaving more like Gardner
than her political opponent!

Table 6.9 Relative frequency of different categories of interruption in
televised political interviews

Speaker$_1$ — Speaker$_2$	Simple interr.	Overlap	Butting-in interr.	Silent interr.	All interr.
Thatcher — Tuohy	4	4	11	0	19
Tuohy — Thatcher	1	8	0	1	10
Callaghan — Gardner	4	6	4	0	14
Gardner — Callaghan	8	11	4	0	23
	17	29	19	1	66

Table 6.9 shows how the different categories of interruption varied
across interview and speaker. Overlaps were the most frequent form
of interruption, and silent interruptions the least frequent. (Only
Margaret Thatcher used silent interruptions, and then only one.)
Interestingly, in the study of interruption in university tutorials
reported earlier, I also found there that overlaps were the most
common form of interruption and silent interruptions the least
common. In these political interviews, overlaps were the most
common form of interruption for all individual speakers except Denis
Tuohy, who displayed a disproportionately large number of butting-in
interruptions. In the Thatcher interview there were 11 cases of
butting-in interruptions when Thatcher held the floor but none when
Tuohy held the floor. In the other interview Callaghan and Gardner
produced exactly equal numbers of butting-in interruptions (i.e. 4).
The high frequency of butting-in interruptions by Tuohy when
Thatcher held the floor is perhaps the most striking aspect of these
data.

If one compares the frequency with which the two interviews
produced butting-in interruptions as opposed to other kinds of
interruption using standard statistical procedures, the difference tends
towards but narrowly fails to reach significance, largely because of the
small numbers involved ($x^2 = 2.89$, d.f. = 1, $p < 0.01$).

One interesting point is that although the overall number of
interruptions produced by the politicians does not exceed the number
produced by their interviewers (33 in each case), the number of

overlaps produced by the politicians is almost double the number produced by the interviewers (19 as opposed to 10). Ferguson (1977), of course, found that overlaps were the form of interruption that was the most reliable index of dominance. In university tutorials overlaps were more significantly used by tutors than students, again suggesting that this form of behaviour reflects dominance.

In the Discussion, I will consider possible interpretations of the observation of the high frequency of butting-in interruptions by Denis Tuohy when Margaret Thatcher held the floor. But first I want to discuss some other aspects of the two politicians' speech that will probably have some bearing on this issue. Using the pauseometer and Nascom microcomputer I analysed samples of speech of the two politicians from the beginning, middle, and end of the interviews. The computer program gave me a reading of the total duration of unfilled pauses ($\geq$ 200 milliseconds, Boomer 1965): in the speech sample, the total duration of phonation, and the total length of the sample (as well as the switching-pause, but this is not relevant here). The speech was then transcribed and the number of words counted. From these measures the speech rate and articulation rate were calculated (see Goldman-Eisler 1968, chapter 1). Table 6.10 shows the speech rate and articulation rate of the two politicians estimated at different points in the interview. Again, some interesting differences emerge – Callaghan's speech rate and articulation rate decline steadily throughout the course of the interview. On the other hand, Margaret Thatcher's speech rate and articulation rate reach their maximum in the middle of the interview. Callaghan starts fast and get slower. Thatcher needs some time to warm up. However, even after Margaret Thatcher has warmed up, her articulation rate and speech rate never exceed Callaghan's lowest limits!

Table 6.10 Speech rate and articulation rate of Margaret Thatcher and Jim Callaghan (in words/min)

Stage of interview	Margaret Thatcher		Jim Callaghan	
	Speech rate	Articulation rate	Speech rate	Articulation rate
Beginning	167.4	181.9	220.9	241.4
Middle	184.0	202.1	207.8	223.2
End	174.5	189.8	196.1	212.7
Mean	175.5	191.4	207.3	224.5

There are also striking differences in the incidence of filled pauses in the speech of the two politicians. Filled pauses (ah, er, um, etc.) have been hypothesized to possess a floor-holding function, in addition to making time for cognitive planning in speech (Maclay and Osgood 1959; Ball 1975; Beattie 1977; Beattie and Barnard 1979). Margaret Thatcher, in her interview, only used four in the whole time, whereas Callaghan used 22 (Gardner used 20, and Tuohy 10). Undoubtedly Callaghan's high speech rate is an important determinant of his higher filled pause rate, but it should be emphasized that Callaghan's filled pause rate is much closer to the norm than Margaret Thatcher's. Four filled pauses in a 25-minute interview is remarkably few.

DISCUSSION

This study focussing on turn-taking and interruptions in televised political interviews has produced some evidence of significant differences in interview behaviour between Margaret Thatcher and Jim Callaghan. Margaret Thatcher is interrupted by her interviewer almost twice as often as she interrupts him. Jim Callaghan, on the other hand, interrupts his interviewer more than he himself is interrupted. Both politicians use overlaps most frequently, and they use this form of interruption almost twice as often as their interviewers. Overlaps, which are interruptions involving simultaneous speech but in which the interrupted person manages to apparently complete his or her turn, were the only form of interruption found by Ferguson (1977) to correlate with self-ratings of dominance. I found that overlaps were used significantly more frequently by tutors than by students in university tutorials. The present study again suggests that this form of interruption acts as a subtle reflection of dominance relationships in conversation.

Perhaps the most surprising and counterintuitive finding of this study is that Margaret Thatcher is interrupted significantly more frequently in her interview than Callaghan is in his. Earlier I reviewed the evidence that turn-taking style is likely to be influential in interpersonal perception and that with the televised political interview, in which the intimate conversational behaviour of politicians is witnessed by millions of observers, there are likely to be strong beliefs developing about the character and personality of politicians on the basis of conversational behaviour. However, we seem to have a paradox. There is undoubtedly a widespread view among the general public that Margaret Thatcher is domineering in interviews, whereas Callaghan is generally viewed as relaxed and affable. However, the analyses of the interviews revealed that Jim Callaghan interrupts his interviewer more than Margaret Thatcher interrupts hers, and moreover, that Margaret Thatcher's interviewer interrupts her more frequently than she interrupts him. Where, then, does the perception of Thatcher as domineering arise from? One possible suggestion is that it is her determination not to yield the floor when interrupted that leads to this perception. I have already discussed how her speech is punctuated by butting-in interruptions from her interviewer. What is striking about some of these interruptions and other interruptions where she holds the floor is their length.

When interrupted, Margaret Thatcher often tries to finish her point regardless of the duration of simultaneous talking required. Sacks *et al.* (1974) make the point that 'occurrences of more than one party speaking simultaneously are common, but brief'. Beattie and Barnard (1979) reported that the mean duration of simultaneous speech in face-to-face conversation is 454 milliseconds. In the Thatcher interview, however, some periods of simultaneous speech last for as long as 5 seconds.

In the example below, the italicized words were spoken simultaneously by Margaret Thatcher and Denis Tuohy. Tuohy started speaking in the juncture after the second 'society'.

MT: . . . there are comparatively few people / they could be measured in thousands / who wish to destroy the kind of society which you and I value / destroy the free society / *Please, please this is the most please this is the most please this is* / the most important point you have raised / There are people in this country who are the great destroyers.

DT: *You were talking about striking ambulance workers you were talking about ancilliary workers in hospitals*

Margaret Thatcher often wins the battle for the floor when she is interrupted, as can be seen from the high proportion of butting-in interruptions in her speech (i.e. interruptions in which the interrupter Denis Tuohy does not gain the floor), and it is perhaps for this reason that television viewers perceive her as domineering. What viewers often fail to notice is that it is not she but her interviewer who interrupts in the first place.

An important question, of course, is why she is interrupted so frequently in the first place. One hypothesis, which, following Zimmerman and West (1975), might be termed the 'male dominance' hypothesis, is that there is some evidence that women are interrupted more frequently than men; and Margaret Thatcher, despite being leader of the Opposition at the time of the interview, with all the power that goes with it, is still fundamentally a woman, to be dominated by men. This hypothesis would maintain that Margaret Thatcher and Denis Tuohy are simply displaying behaviours typical of women and men, respectively. This, of course, could easily be tested, by investigating whether Tuohy interrupts other women to a similar degree. My guess is that there is probably something else going on here. The cause of the high frequency of interruption in Margaret Thatcher's speech may lie in the prosodic and nonverbal behaviours that regulate conversation. Duncan identified six turn-yielding cues (rising/falling intonation, drawl on final syllable or stressed syllable of a terminal clause, sociocentric sequence, drop in pitch or loudness on a sociocentric sequence, syntactic clause completion, and gesture termination). He demonstrated that the higher the conjoint frequency of these cues, the greater is the probability of a listener turn-taking attempt (although one should perhaps have some reservations about the magnitude of the correlation claimed, see Chapter 5). He also posited the existence of attempt suppression signals that could override the effects of any number of turn-yielding cues. The only attempt suppression signal he actually identified was speaker gesticulation, and he demonstrated that when the speaker was actually engaged in gesture, the incidence of listener turn-taking attempts fell virtually to zero. Another possible attempt suppression signal that has been identified is the filled pause (ah, er, um, etc.). Ball (1975), for example, found that filled pauses effectively delayed subjects taking the floor in conversational dyads. Beattie (1977) also showed that filled pauses reduced the probability of a speaker-switch, at least for a short period after their occurrence.

Mrs Thatcher may be interruped frequently because she unintentionally sends out a set of prosodic and nonverbal turn-yielding cues that result in an attempted speaker-switch. Many of the interruptions of Margaret Thatcher that occurred in this interview were found at the ends of clauses in her speech in which there was drawl on the stressed syllable in the clause and there was a falling intonation pattern associated with the end of the clause. Duncan has identified all three of these as turn-yielding cues. Margaret Thatcher does not seem to display attempt suppression signals that could override the effects of these cues. In the whole Thatcher interview I found that Margaret Thatcher only used 4 filled pauses in all, while Tuohy used 10. (Callaghan used 22 in his, and Gardner 20.) She often uses a hand gesture only after the interruption has begun. Consider the following exchange between Margaret Thatcher and Denis Tuohy.

MT: The police do a fantastic job
DT: Coming
MT: and we must support them in every way possible.
DT: Coming towards the end of our time, Mrs Thatcher . . .

Denis Tuohy starts to speak after Mrs Thatcher says 'job'. This might seem to be an appropriate point to begin, because it is the end of a syntactic clause, there is drawl on the stressed middle syllable of 'fantastic', and there is a final-sounding intonation associated with the end of the clause. Denis Tuohy seems to think that Mrs Thatcher has finished and begins to speak. A filled pause after 'job' might have been appropriate in signalling that there was more speech to come and that the combination of vocal cues did not constitute an appropriate point for a speaker-switch. One may only speculate that the speech training Margaret Thatcher has received may have in part contributed to this problem. But can we test experimentally this hypothesis, that Mrs Thatcher is often interrupted because she displays turn-yielding cues at inappropriate places?

Figure 6.2 It <u>just</u> can't

Figure 6.3 Yes <u>it can</u> tell you

Figure 6.4 <u>But</u> the second point is this

Figure 6.5 <u>It's valu</u>able all round

Figure 6.6 <u>and he</u> did

Figure 6.7 <u>One mo</u>ment, one moment

Figure 6.8 One moment, <u>one</u> moment

Figure 6.9 Well can I just answer

With Anne Cutler and Mark Pearson from Sussex University, I designed a series of experiments to try to test this hypothesis (see Beattie, Cutler and Pearson 1982). Forty extracts were selected from the Denis Tuohy *TV Eye* interview – ten were turn-final (i.e. utterances at the end of a turn immediately preceding a smooth speaker-switch), twenty were turn-medial (i.e. utterances from within a turn), and the remaining ten were turn-disputed (utterances immediately preceding an interruption by Tuohy). These extracts all contained at least one sentence. The extracts were presented to subjects who had to judge whether Mrs Thatcher's turn was complete or not, in a forced-choice procedure. The extracts were presented on video to 79 subjects, on audio only to 29 subjects (in the audio presentation, only the final tone group or phonemic clause of each utterance was presented, with 2 exceptions in which the last 2 tone groups were played because the final tone group comprised only one word), on vision only to 14 subjects and typescripts of the extracts were presented to 20 subjects. There were different numbers of subjects in conditions because the extracts were presented in university classes. All subjects were students at the Universities of Sheffield or Sussex. For each of the 40 extracts in each of the 4 modes of presentation, the percentages of completion judgements were calculated (see Table 6.11a).

An analysis of variance revealed that both Type of Utterance (turn-final, etc.) ($F = 23.265$; $p < 0.0001$) and Mode of Presentation ($F = 8.282$, $p < 0.0001$) significantly affected judgements of completion. There was also a significant interaction effect between type of utterance and mode of presentation ($F = 7.692$; $p < 0.001$). As predicted, turn-final utterances produced the most completion judgements, and the turn-medial the lowest, with the disputed turns falling somewhere in between these two. One-factor ANOVAs revealed that Type of Utterance had a significant effect in the case of the video presentation ($F = 34.791$, $p < 0.0001$), audio presentation ($F = 5.129$, $p < 0.02$) and vision-only presentation ($F = 25.486$, $p < 0.001$). With the typescript, however, there was no significant effect ($F = 1.185$, n.s.). (It should be noted that significant effects did

Table 6.11a Mean percentage of utterances judged to be complete

	Mode of presentation			
	Video	*Vision only*	*Audio only*	*Typescript*
Turn-final	83.530	76.430	62.230	63.500
Turn-disputed	40.120	38.570	55.860	50.500
Turn-medial	23.045	18.570	32.405	58.250

Table 6.11b Correlations between presentation modes (percent completion judgements for each utterance)

Vision only	Audio only	Typescript	
0.898	0.676	0.083	Video
	0.586	0.000	Vision only
		0.080	Audio only

emerge in conditions with smaller numbers of subjects than the typescript condition, thus in fact demonstrating the robustness of the effects.) A comparison of means, using the Tukey HSD procedure (Winer, 1962, p. 87), revealed that judged completion scores were significantly higher for turn-disputed utterances than for turn-medial utterances for the video presentation (F = 5.53, $p < 0.05$), the audio presentation (F = 5.15, $p < 0.05$), and the vision-only presentation (F = 6.09, $p < 0.05$).

Tests for correlation revealed significant positive correlations (all at the 0.001 level or beyond) among the video, vision-only and audio-only conditions for proportion of completion judgements for each utterance. The typescript condition judgements, however, did not correlate significantly with any of the other conditions (see Table 6.11b). Thus, although, for example, the means for the turn-final utterances in the audio and typescript conditions are similar, the individual utterance ratings which comprise the means are obviously quite different.

In other words, the basic hypothesis was supported – those utterances immediately preceding an interruption by the interviewer were judged to be complete more often than turn-medial utterances and this was not on the basis of syntactic or semantic content (present in the typescript) because of course no significant effect emerged in the case of the typescript, but on the basis of information carried in the audio channel and in the visual channel of the interaction, as models of turn-taking such as that of Duncan would predict. Subsequent analyses sought to determine exactly which signals were giving rise to subjects' perceptions of these utterances as complete.

Firstly, the forty extracts from the Denis Tuohy interview with Mrs Thatcher were digitized and coded into LPC (Linear Predictive Coding) parameters, and a value for the fundamental frequency of each sample extracted. All the forty utterances terminated in a pitch fall with one exception, a question which ended in a rise; this exception was excluded from further auditory analysis. The value of the fundamental frequency in cycles per second was determined for the highest and lowest points (peak and trough) of each terminal fall. The mean values for the three types of utterance are displayed in the first two columns of Table 6.12. The third column shows the mean pitch range covered by the fall (i.e. the difference between columns one and two), and the fourth column gives the mean time in milliseconds over which the fall was realized.

Unequal-N analyses of variance on these four measures showed that on two of them, the three conditions differed significantly:
(a) The trough of the fall: the difference between conditions was

Table 6.12 Mean peak and trough values for three types of utterance

	Peak	*Trough*	△	*Span*
Turn-final	238 Hz	141 Hz	97 Hz	693 msec.
Turn-disputed	263 Hz	167 Hz	96 Hz	463 msec.
Turn-medial	275 Hz	161 Hz	114 Hz	953 msec.

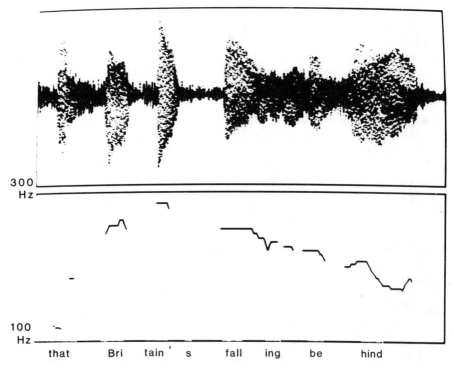

Figure 6.10 Amplitude trace and pitch contour of turn-medial utterance, showing slow fall in utterance pitch

significant (F = 5.75, $p < 0.01$), and Scheffé post-hoc comparisons showed that the turn-final utterances ended significantly lower than the other two groups, which did not differ significantly from one another.

(b) The timespan over which the terminal fall was realized: the difference between conditions was significant (F = 4.61, $p < 0.02$), and Scheffé post-hoc comparisons showed that this effect was due to the turn-medial falls being slower than either of the other two types of utterance, which did not differ significantly. There was no significant difference between the three types of utterance on either the height of the pitch peak or the range of the fall.

This analysis suggests that the turn-disputed utterances may, in fact, have conflicting cues: a fast fall like the turn-final utterances, but a fall which does not descend very low, like the turn-medial utterances. This, in turn, suggests that while the speaker is actually giving a number of cues to the end of her turn, the cue which she

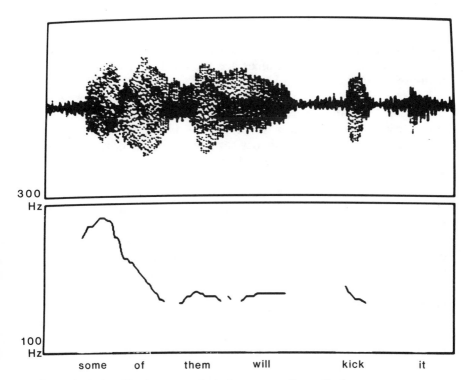

Figure 6.11 Amplitude trace and pitch contour of turn-final utterance, showing fast fall in utterance pitch

considers paramount may be different from the cue which her interlocutor considers paramount. If she considered that her most decisive cue to the end of her turn was letting her voice drop to around 140 Hz instead of keeping it no lower than 160 Hz, whereas her interlocutor considered that her most decisive cue was a rapidly executed final fall rather than a slow fall, then their respective decisions as to whether or not she had finished her turn would differ in precisely those cases which were disputed in the present sample of utterances.

Mark Pearson, trained in phonetic transcription, then transcribed the forty utterances, without knowledge of the position of the utterances in the speaker's turn. The transcriptions of the turn-final and turn-medial utterances were then separately inspected, and the prosodic and vocal quality features occurring in three or more of these utterances listed. Five 'final' features were found: pitch downstep (rapid drop) before the main fall (tonic); double falling contour; allegro portion prior to the tonic; whispery voice; and creaky voice. Three 'medial' features were found: allegro continuing through the tonic; pitch upstep before the final fall; and a non-falling sustained contour after the fall. (Note that because all our sample utterances ended in falls, we must have underestimated the complete range of cues when non-falling utterances are included. For example, many turn-medial utterances end in a fall–rise.)

The remaining utterances were then checked for the presence of these features, which were assumed to be characteristic of turn-final and turn-medial utterances respectively. The five 'final' features occurred on average 2.2 times per turn-final utterance, but 0.2 times per turn-medial utterance. Turn-disputed utterances, with a mean of 1.6, are closer to the turn-final utterances than to the turn-medial utterances. The three 'medial' cues occurred on average 0.65 times per turn-medial utterance, but 0.10 times per turn-final utterance. Turn-disputed utterances again fell in between with a mean of 0.30.

The number of acoustic cues present in each utterance was then correlated with the results of the audio perception test, and the proportion of completion judgements for each utterance was found to have a significant positive correlation with the mean number of 'final' cues present in that utterance ($r = 0.46$, $p = 0.003$), but a significant negative correlation with the mean number of 'medial' cues ($r = -0.45$, $p = 0.004$). Thus, the listeners in this experiment appear to have been making use of these phonetic and vocal quality cues in making their forced-choice judgements.

In terms of the visual channel, the main signal guiding completion judgements must have been eye-gaze since, in a large proportion of instances, the camera angle was such that no information was available on other aspects of nonverbal behaviour such as gesture (gesture termination being an important turn-yielding signal, and gesture maintenance an important attempt-suppression signal, according to Duncan). Eye-gaze has been shown in the past to be implicated in turn regulation. Analysis of the video revealed that in 100% of the turn-final utterances, Mrs Thatcher was looking at her interviewer at the end of the utterance, compared with 55% of turn-medial utterances. Turn-disputed utterances were again in between with 80%.

This study indeed produced evidence that interruptions in Mrs Thatcher's interviews are related to the occurrence of certain features in her speech and behaviour. A number of the turn-yielding cues identified by Duncan (1972) do predict the onset of interviewer responses in her televised interviews.

Conclusions

In this chapter I explored some of the variables that seem to affect interruption in conversation. In the first study of non-dyadic tutorials the frequency of different types of interruptions was shown to be related to a number of social variables. The status of interactants but not their sex was shown to have a significant effect on the number and types of interruption that arose. Tutors tended to overlap with students more than vice versa. This is a type of interruption which, as I have already said, requires considerable psycholinguistic skill demanding as it does the ability to predict a possible completion point. Students, on the other hand, used simple interruptions more frequently than tutors. These are interruptions which occur in the middle of utterances. This study of interruptions was in many ways a very preliminary investigation, but nevertheless it does have important implications. Perhaps the main one is that quite simply interruptions are not a unitary, homogeneous phenomenon. There are different types, and the different types are employed certainly by different people and probably for different functions (although this latter issue remains to be explored). This finding has very important repercussions for clinical psychology and other disciplines which have worked with undifferentiated measures of interruption.

In the second study of political interviews, it was shown that some interruptions can arise, not because interactants wish to dominate or disrupt a conversation, but through a misinterpretation of the signals which guide the regulation of conversation. This second investigation provided further support for the efficacy of the cues identified by Duncan (1972) and discussed in Chapter 5. Mrs Thatcher's political interviews provide strong support for the hypothesis that syntax but more especially intonation guide and control turn-taking in conversation.

7

Conclusions

Every attempt to explain human behaviour, especially the irrational, must as a matter of course end in simplification.

MORTON SEIDEN

'The Paradox of Hate: A Study in Ritual Murder' (1967)

In this book I have described a series of studies into the analysis of language and nonverbal communication in their natural domain – conversation. I began (in Chapter 3) with a fundamental psycholinguistic question – what is the basic encoding unit in spontaneous speech? The method chosen for answering this question was the examination of the temporal properties of spontaneous language. The method was not a novel one; it was first proposed by Lounsbury (1954) some three decades ago. The distinctive feature of the methodology here, however, was that the spontaneous speech analysed was taken from dialogue rather than from monologue. The rationale behind this was simple. Monologue is a more uncommon event. Speech, when it does occur, nearly always springs up within the context of conversation. Whatever cognitive processes mediate and generate spontaneous speech, they must be sufficiently flexible to operate successfully in conversation. Conversation imposes constraints on the temporal aspects of language. One obvious example of this is that very long pauses within a turn are generally kept to a minimum in conversation. Monologue, however, imposes no such constraints. It is, in passing, informative to consider the maximum length of pause reported in studies of the temporal aspects of language which have used either monologues or dialogues. In the early pioneering studies of

Goldman-Eisler (1958a, 1958b), in which the *majority* of samples of spontaneous speech were taken from dialogue situations (interviews or debates), the longest pause observed was 6.0 seconds, whereas in the Hawkins (1973) study of class and language in which the speech was from a monologue (a story to a teddy bear), the longest pause was 67.1 seconds. In conversation, pauses of more than one minute within a turn would be so striking that the conversation would probably terminate or rapidly change course as a result of embarrassment. The process of turn-taking alone in conversation acts as a guarantee that such pauses will not crop up with any frequency. In monologues, speakers have the privilege of drifting off now and then – as they undoubtedly did in the Hawkins study because the long temporal delays observed were not in any way associated with an improvement in linguistic performance; in conversations, speakers have no such privilege.

For these basic reasons I chose to study the temporal aspects of language in dialogue, the type of dialogue chosen being university supervisions. The reason for this specific choice was that these dyadic conversations between a tutor and a student occur naturally within a psychological laboratory, indeed, in this particular case, often within the very room in which the recording was made. It seemed preferable at the outset to obtain speech samples which were reasonably natural rather than to bring subjects into the laboratory for the express purpose of holding a conversation.

The analysis of the temporal properties of language revealed two fundamental patterns. Temporal cycles with a mean duration of approximately 22 seconds were observed. These cycles had been first described by Henderson *et al.* (1966). They seemed to constitute units which are primarily semantic (see Butterworth 1975) and syntactically larger than individual sentences. But in addition, the analysis of the temporal properties of speech revealed an apparently functional connection between hesitations and clausal units within certain periods of speech. It was observed that there was a relationship between clause length and the probability and duration of a hesitation but only within the so-called 'hesitant phases' of the larger temporal cycles. No such relationship was observed during the fluent phases of cycles.

Another advantage of using conversation as the primary source of data is that it is possible to analyse the nonverbal accompaniments of speech. In conversation, speakers sometimes look at their interlocutor, sometimes they do not. In Chapter 3 I reported an experiment which demonstrated that a speaker's direct gaze at the listener interferes with the planning of spontaneous speech. Speakers seem to avert eye-gaze when planning is occurring. In the search for encoding units of spontaneous speech, analysis of speakers' gaze direction was a powerful additional tool. I discovered that speakers tended to avert eye-gaze at clause juncture pauses in the hesitant phases of temporal cycles. They did so much less frequently during clause juncture pauses in the fluent phases of temporal cycles. These observations supported the hesitation analyses. Certain juncture pauses appear to be used for cognitive planning; others do not. The psycholinguistic model which seemed to emerge from the data was one in which some (probably semantic) suprasentential planning does occur but one in which planning on a clausal basis also occurs (see also Beattie 1980c). Speakers seem to generate speech on a clause-by-clause basis whilst they are generating their semantic plan for the next run of clauses (8.80 clauses being the average length of the cycles). When one considers the demands of conversation, the model would seem intuitively reasonable. Its flexibility allows speakers to be coherent (that is to say, have sufficient time to plan speech in advance) without losing the floor.

Chapter 4 focussed on the organization of nonverbal behaviour within longer turns (that is those of 30 seconds or more) within the same types of conversation. It used the psycholinguistic model, developed in Chapter 3, to provide the basic framework. It described the patterning of eye-gaze and gesture with respect to the types of unit isolated in Chapter 3. Speaker gaze at the listener was found to be organized within a coordinated system with the temporal cycles, with gaze being more common in the more fluent phases of cycles. When speakers did monitor the listener during the apparent planning phases of the temporal cycles, there was a marked increment in the amount of filled hesitations and particularly false starts in speech. This supports the observation made in Chapter 3 and again points towards the basic incompatibility of monitoring a listener, and planning spontaneous speech. Speaker hand movement and gesture also displayed character-istic patterns with respect to the temporal cycles. Batonic movements, that is simple stress-timed movements, were most common in periods of phonation in the hesitant phases of cycles, whereas the more complex iconic gestures were most common accompanying relatively unpredictable content words and beginning in pauses in the fluent phases of cycles. These results suggest that only in fluent phases of temporal cycles is there some semantic specification of certain content words available in advance of the word actually being uttered (as revealed through the iconic nature of the gesture). It was also demonstrated that changes in the basic equilibrium position of the arms and hands tended to coincide with the clause junctures nearest the ends of the temporal cycles. Speaker gaze at the listener at such junctures was also very high (nearly 82% of the time). Since both of these types of nonverbal cues *can* act in conversation to inform the listener that it is their turn to speak, and since they were found at the ends of the temporal cycles, it is suggested that temporal cycles as well as being primary units in terms of the psycholinguistic aspects of language, are also primary units in the organization of conversational exchanges.

In Chapter 5 attention was switched from the organization of behaviour within turns to the organizational principles which connect turns within conversation. A number of different models of the process were presented and evaluated. The two principle models are, from within psychology, that of Duncan (1972) and elaborated in Duncan and Fiske (1977), and, from outside psychology, that of Sacks, Schegloff and Jefferson (1974). As I pointed out there are few points of contact between these two models. Sacks *et al.* concentrate on an analysis of the role of language in turn-taking. They work primarily with audio-recordings. They use common-sense knowledge to unravel the processes. No statistical evidence is presented and the issue of reliability of measurement is not confronted — except to the extent that the reader agrees (or not) with the conversational analyst's own intuitions about the examples provided and discussed. Starkey Duncan's method differs considerably from that of the ethnomethodologists. He worked with a small number of video-recordings of interaction. The interactions analysed are those involving people brought into the laboratory for that specific purpose (Sacks *et al.* concentrate on audio-recordings of natural interactions). Duncan analyses nonverbal behaviour as well as some aspects of language — but those aspects of language analysed tend to be discrete features like intonation or syntax — features that can be analysed with reliability by observers, features that do not require the observer of the conversation to evoke many of his or her own intuitions about the pragmatics of discourse in order to understand or analyse it. Not only are there few points of contact between the models but at first glance each would seem to make the other redundant. Sacks *et al.* have described a series of turn-allocation rules which would seem to account successfully for the examples they present. Duncan, on the other hand, has identified a series of cues which he called 'turn-yielding cues' whose conjoint frequency seems to predict very well the probability of the listener taking the floor smoothly (that is without simultaneous turn-claimings). A correlation of 0.96 is claimed in the original paper (Duncan, 1972) to exist between the number of turn-yielding cues conjointly displayed and the probability of the listener taking the floor. Duncan also identified one cue (the maintenance of a hand gesture) which can override the effects of these cues, indeed virtually eliminating the possibility of the listener taking the floor. Both models appear highly successful but both cannot be correct. If turn-taking is purely predictable on the basis of an arithmetical adding of discrete cues then the rules elucidated by Sacks *et al.* are not necessary. In Chapter 5 I report some of my own observations of conversation which have direct bearing on these issues. In the first study employing objective analysis of the temporal properties of natural telephone conversations I discovered that turn-taking on the telephone appears to be remarkably smooth, quick and efficient. Speakers exchange the floor with minimum delay and with little simultaneous speech. These data are compatible with both models since both place a good deal of emphasis on information carried in the auditory channel for turn-taking. However, these data are not compatible with the earlier psychological accounts such as that of Kendon (1967), which placed total emphasis on the role of visually-transmitted signals in the regulation of conversation. I then reported some data from dyadic academic conversations, which involved the analysis of the discrete turn-yielding cues described by Duncan, and the relationship between these and smooth transitions in conversation (and transitions mediated by simultaneous turn-claimings). These cues were a good predictor of the smooth exchange of turns but not exactly as Duncan had suggested. The linear relationship between number of discrete turn-yielding cues and the probability of a listener turn-taking attempt suggested by Duncan was not replicated (indeed I suggest in Chapter 5 that the original correlation of 0.96 may be statistically suspect anyway). In my data, special cue combinations (a model explicitly rejected by Duncan and Fiske 1977, see p. 200) were the best predictor of listener smooth turn-taking attempts. Clause completion accompanied by a falling intonation with drawl on the stressed syllable seems to operate effectively in conversation to inform the listener that it is their turn to speak. These cues may be accompanied by the termination of a hand gesture. I provided further evidence of this in Chapter 6 when I demonstrated that in political interviews Mrs Thatcher is interrupted at points where she displays this combination of cues. In that study with Anne Cutler and Mark Pearson we were even able to quantify the precise nature of the intonational cue. The major auditory cue she was sending was a fast-fall intonation at the end of a tone group. In her interviews her interlocutor often responds to this cue even when she apparently has not finished talking. What is interesting about my attempt to replicate Duncan's research is that the special cue combination model now being proposed could be worked into the Sacks *et al.* framework. Special cue combinations could easily demarcate the kinds of linguistic and pragmatic units that Sacks *et al.* discussed. They do after all recognize the importance of features like intonation – indeed they say 'any word can be made into a "one-word" unit type via intonation' (1974, p. 722), where a one-word unit-type would constitute a basic unit of interaction, but they do not go on to explore exactly how intonation could do this. In the Thatcher study reported in Chapter 6 there is perhaps a hint of the way forward. To understand discourse our common-sense understanding is relevant and indeed necessary but this need not exclude scientific precision and reliability. Intonation can be measured with a high degree of precision and with high reliability, and in this book I have reported perhaps the first study of conversation to introduce such clear reliable measures.

In Chapter 5 I also attempted to outline how the organizational principles of nonverbal behaviour described in Chapter 4 may exert an influence on the operation of signals guiding turn-taking. This part of the discussion was somewhat schematic and I simply tried to show how the patterning of eye-gaze will exert an influence on its efficacy as a turn-yielding signal. Speaker gaze does facilitate turn-taking, but only in some specific contexts – those contexts to be understood in psycholinguistic terms as periods of planning in speech, periods characterized by high levels of gaze aversion.

Chapter 6 reported some preliminary investigations of interruptions in conversation: for the first time, conversations were reported involving more than two people. These again were academic in nature but can, I feel, be justified in exactly the same way as the earlier ones were. Chapter 6 differs in terms of approach from the earlier studies because it does not attempt to explain interruptions with respect to what they do in the interaction, that is to say in terms of the future organization of the interaction, but instead seeks to connect the occurrence of some of these interruptions to the social characteristics of the people concerned. If all of the investigations reported in this book are preliminary and exploratory, Chapter 6 must be seen as a preliminary to a preliminary. The study on tutorial groups nevertheless reveals some interesting and perhaps surprising results. The widely publicized result of Zimmerman and West (1975), that men constantly dominate women in conversation by interrupting them, was not replicated. Sex of participant played little role in the dynamics of the conversation, but status did. Tutors were found to use a higher proportion of that specific type of interruption which has in the past been shown to correlate with ratings of 'dominance' than did students. The type of interruption concerned was overlap. Here the tutors begin speaking simultaneously with the student at a possible completion point (cf. the 'transition relevance places' of Sacks *et al.*). Overlaps hinge on a basic psycholinguistic competence – they are essentially predictive. Tutors must be able to anticipate possible completion points and have preplanned some of their own speech in turn. Overlaps in conversation reflect some of the most basic psycholinguistic skills that interactants bring to bear in a conversation. The rest of Chapter 6 was devoted to an exploration of the interview patterns of some senior politicians and particularly Mrs Margaret Thatcher, the Prime Minister of Britain. Interruptions in her speech were shown to be connected to the display of cues first identified by Duncan, and discussed in detail in Chapter 5. Margaret Thatcher is interrupted a good deal and she is a woman, but I think the evidence suggests that the interruptions have little to do with her sex *per se*.

This book is a report on a research endeavour, an endeavour which is not complete, indeed an endeavour which has only just begun. The focus of the research so far has been narrow. I have concentrated largely on academic discussions and political interviews because they are samples which are easy to obtain and they do not owe their existence to the presence of the conversational analyst. I have tried to show how some consideration of the basic psycholinguistic processes which underlie spontaneous speech is relevant to the understanding of conversation. Conversation is after all two or more people speaking (usually) spontaneously in each other's presence but it involves more than mere talk. In conversations, our minds and our bodies become uniquely engaged. Conversations involve the whole person. In this book, I have tried to unravel some of the important connections between processes of the mind and processes of the body (i.e. nonverbal behaviour). Psycholinguists will say that I have over-simplified many of the basic processes; conversational analysts will say that I have been too restrictive in what I have tried to explain. I apologize to both groups and take refuge with Henry Adams' famous quotation:

Simplicity is the most deceitful mistress that ever betrayed man
('The Education of Henry Adams,' 1907)

References

Aborn, M., Rubenstein, H. and Sterling, T. D. (1959) Sources of contextual constraint upon words in sentences, *Journal of Experimental Psychology* **57**, 171–80.

Allport, D. A. (1980) Attention and performance, in G. L. Claxton (ed.), *New Directions in Cognitive Psychology*, London: Routledge & Kegan Paul.

Anderson, B. J. (1977) The emergence of conversational behaviour, *Journal of Communication*27, 85–91.

Anderson, B. J. and Vietze, P. (1977) Early dialogues: the structure of reciprocal infant–mother vocalization, in S. Cohen and T. J. Comiskey (eds.), *Child Development: A Study of Growth Processes* (2nd end), Illinois: Peacock.

Argyle, M. (1967) *The Psychology of Interpersonal Behaviour*, Harmondsworth: Penguin.

Argyle, M. (1970) Eye contact and distance: A reply to Stephenson and Rutter, *British Journal of Psychology* **61**, 395–6.

Argyle, M. (1974) *Social Interaction*, London: Methuen.

Argyle, M. (1975) *Bodily Communication*, London: Methuen.

Argyle, M. (1978) Non-verbal communication and mental disorder, *Psychological Medicine* **23**, 551–4.

Argyle, M., Alkema, F. and Gilmour, R. (1971) The communication of friendly and hostile attitudes by verbal and nonverbal signals, *European Journal of Social Psychology* **1**, 385–402.

Argyle, M. and Cook, M. (1976) *Gaze and Mutual Gaze*, Cambridge: Cambridge University Press.

Argyle, M. and Dean, J. (1965) Eye-contact, distance and affiliation, *Sociometry* **28**, 289–304.

Argyle, M. and Ingham, R. (1972) Gaze, mutual gaze and proximity, *Semiotica* **1**, 32–49.

Argyle, M. and Kendon, A. (1967) The experimental analysis of social performance, in L. Berkowitz (ed.), *Advances in Experimental Social Psychology*, vol. 3, New York: Academic Press.

Argyle, M., Lefebvre, L. and Cook, M. (1974) The meaning of five patterns of gaze, *European Journal of Social Psychology* **4**, 125–36.

Argyle, M., Salter, V., Nicholson, H., Williams, M. and Burgess, P. (1970) The communication of inferior and superior attitudes by verbal and non-verbal signals, *British Journal of Social and Clinical Psychology* **9**, 222–31.

Argyle, M. and Trower, P. (1979) *Person to Person: Ways of Communicating*, London: Harper and Row.

Ball, P. (1975) Listener responses to filled pauses in relation to floor apportionment, *British Journal of Social and Clinical Psychology* **14**, 423–4.

Barik, H. C. (1968) On defining juncture pauses: a note on Boomer's 'Hesitation and grammatical encoding', *Language and Speech* **11**, 156–9.

Barnard, P. J. (1974) Unpublished corpus of 800 directory enquiry conversations.

Bateson, G. (1973) *Steps to an Ecology of Mind*, St Albans: Paladin.

Baxter, J. C., Winters, E. P. and Hammer, R. E. (1968) Gestural behaviour during a brief interview as a function of cognitive variables, *Journal of Personality and Social Psychology* **8**, 303–7.

Beattie, G. W. (1977) The dynamics of interruption and the filled pause, *British Journal of Social and Clinical Psychology* **16**, 283–4.

Beattie, G. W. (1978a) Floor apportionment and gaze in conversational dyads, *British Journal of Social and Clinical Psychology* **17**, 7–16.

Beattie, G. W. (1978b) Sequential temporal patterns of speech and gaze in dialogue, *Semiotica* **23**, 29–52.

Beattie, G. W. (1979a) Planning units in spontaneous speech: some evidence from hesitation in speech and speaker gaze direction, in conversation, *Linguistics* **17**, 61–78.

Beattie, G. W. (1979b) Contextual constraints on the floor-apportionment function of gaze in dyadic conversation, *British Journal of Social and Clinical Psychology* **18**, 391–2.

Beattie, G. W. (1979c) The 'Troubles' in Northern Ireland, *Bulletin of the British Psychological Society* **32**, 249–52.

Beattie, G. W. (1979d) The modifiability of the temporal structure of spontaneous speech, in A. W. Siegman and S. Feldstein (eds.), *Of Speech and Time: Temporal Speech Patterns in Interpersonal Contexts*, New Jersey: Laurence Erlbaum.

Beattie, G. W. (1979e) Reflections on *Reflections on Language* by Noam Chomsky, *Linguistics* **17**, 907–23.

Beattie, G. W. (1980a) The skilled art of conversational interaction: verbal and nonverbal signals in its regulation and management, in W. T. Singleton, P. Spurgeon and R. B. Stammers (eds.), *The Analysis of Social Skill*, New York: Plenum.

Beattie, G. W. (1980b) The role of language production processes in the organization of behaviour in face-to-face interaction, in B. Butterworth (ed.), *Language Production, Speech and Talk*, vol. 1, London: Academic Press.

Beattie, G. W. (1980c) Encoding units in spontaneous speech: some implications for the dynamics of conversation, in H. W. Dechert and M. Raupach (eds.), *Temporal Variables in Speech: Studies in Honour of Frieda Goldman-Eisler*, The Hague: Mouton.

Beattie, G. W. (1981a) A further investigation of the cognitive interference hypothesis of gaze patterns during conversation, *British Journal of Social Psychology* 20, 243–8.

Beattie, G. W. (1981b) The regulation of speaker-turns in face-to-face conversation: some implications for conversation in sound-only communication channels, *Semiotica* 34, 55–70.

Beattie, G. W. (1981c) Interruption in conversational interaction, and its relation to the sex and status of the interactants, *Linguistics* 19, 15–35.

Beattie, G. W. (1982a) Look, just don't interrupt, *New Scientist* 95, 859–60.

Beattie, G. W. (1982b) Turn-taking and interruption in political interviews – Margaret Thatcher and Jim Callaghan compared and contrasted, *Semiotica* 39, 93–114.

Beattie, G. W. and Barnard, P. J. (1979) The temporal structure of natural telephone conversations (directory enquiry calls), *Linguistics* 17, 213–30.

Beattie, G. W. and Bogle, G. (1982) The reliability and validity of different video-recording techniques used for analyzing gaze in dyadic interaction, *British Journal of Social Psychology* 21, 31–4.

Beattie, G. W. and Bradbury, R. J. (1979) An experimental investigation of the modifiability of the temporal structure of spontaneous speech, *Journal of Psycholinguistic Research* 8, 225–48.

Beattie, G. W. and Butterworth, B. L. (1979) Contextual probability and word frequency as determinants of pauses and errors in spontaneous speech, *Language and Speech* 22, 201–11.

Beattie, G. W., Cutler, A. and Pearson, M. (1982) Why is Mrs Thatcher interrupted so often? *Nature* 300, 744–7.

Berry, J. (1953) Some statistical aspects of conversational speech, in W. Jackson (ed.), *Communication Theory*, London: Butterworth.

Birdwhistell, R. L. (1970) *Kinesics and Context: Essays on Body-Motion Communication*, Harmondsworth: Penguin.

Boomer, D. S. (1965) Hesitation and grammatical encoding, *Language and Speech* 8, 148–58.

Boomer, D. S. (1970) Review of F. Goldman-Eisler 'Psycholinguistics: Experiments in Spontaneous Speech', *Lingua* 25, 152–64.

Brooks, W. D. and Emmert, P. (1976) *Interpersonal Communication*, Dubuque, Ia.: Brown.

Bull, P. E. and Brown, R. (1977) The role of postural change in dyadic conversations, *British Journal of Social and Clinical Psychology* 16, 29–33.

Burke, J. P. and Schiavetti, N. (1975) Effects of cumulative context and guessing methods on estimates of transitional probability in speech, *Language and Speech* 4, 299–311.

Burns, K. L. and Beier, E. G. (1973) Significance of vocal and visual channels in the decoding of emotional meaning, *Journal of Communication* 23, 118–30.

Butterworth, B. L. (1972) Semantic analysis of the phasing of fluency in spontaneous speech. Unpublished Ph.D. dissertation, University College London.

Butterworth, B. L. (1975) Hesitation and semantic planning in speech, *Journal of Psycholinguistic Research* **4**, 75–87.

Butterworth, B. L. (1976) Semantic planning, lexical choice and syntactic organization in spontaneous speech. Unpublished paper, University of Cambridge.

Butterworth, B. L. and Beattie, G. W. (1978) Gesture and silence as indicators of planning in speech, in R. N. Campbell and P. T. Smith (eds.), *Recent Advances in the Psychology of Language: Formal and Experimental Approaches*, New York: Plenum.

Butterworth, B., Hine, R. R. and Brady, K. D. (1977) Speech and interaction in sound-only communication channels, *Semiotica* **20**, 81–99.

Campbell, R. N. and Smith, P. T. (eds.), *Recent Advances in the Psychology of Language: Formal and Experimental Approaches*, New York: Plenum.

Chapple, E. D. and Lindemann, E. (1942) Clinical implications of measurements of interacting rates in psychiatric interviews, *Applied Anthropology* **1**, 1–11.

Charny, E. J. (1966) Psychosomatic manifestations of rapport in psychotherapy, *Psychosomatic Medicine* **28**, 305–15.

Chomsky, N. (1965) *Aspects of the Theory of Syntax*, Cambridge, Mass.: MIT Press.

Chomsky, N. (1976) *Reflections on Language*, Glasgow: Fontana.

Chomsky, N. and Halle, M. (1968) *The Sound Pattern of English*, New York: Harper and Row.

Clark, H. H. (1973) The language-as-fixed-effect fallacy: a critique of language statistics in psychological research, *Journal of Verbal Learning and Verbal Behaviour* **12**, 335–59.

Cohen, J. (1960) A coefficient of agreement for nominal scales, *Educational Psychology Measurement* **20**, 37–46.

Condon, W. S. and Ogston, W. D. (1966) Sound film analysis of normal and pathological behavior patterns, *Journal of Nervous and Mental Disease* **143**, 338–47.

Condon, W. S. and Ogston, W. D. (1967) A segmentation of behavior, *Journal of Psychiatric Research* **5**, 221–35.

Cook, M. and Lalljee, M. G. (1972) Verbal substitutes for visual signals in interaction, *Semiotica* **6**, 212–21.

Cook, M. and Smith, J. M. C. (1972) Studies in programmed gaze. Unpublished paper, University College of Swansea.

Cook, M. and Smith, J. M. C. (1975) the role of gaze in impression formation, *British Journal of Social and Clinical Psychology* **14**, 19–25.

Crystal, D. (1975) *The English Tone of Voice*, Bristol: Edward Arnold.

Darwin, C. (1872) *The Expression of Emotion in Man and Animals*, London: Murray.

De Long, A. J. (1974) Kinesic signals at utterance boundaries in pre-school children, *Semiotica* **11**, 43–73.

De Long, A. J. (1975) Yielding the floor: the kinesic signals, *Communication in Infancy and Early Childhood* 1, 98–103.

Deutsch, F. (1947) Analysis of postural behaviour, *Psychoanalytic Quarterly* 16, 195–213.

Deutsch, F. (1952) Analytic posturology, *Psychoanalytic Quarterly* 21, 196–214.

Dittmann, A. T. (1972) The body movement–speech rhythm relationship as a cue to speech encoding, in A. Siegman and B. Pope (eds.), *Studies in Dyadic Communication*, New York: Pergamon.

Dittmann, A. T. and Llewellyn, L. G. (1967) The phonemic clause as a unit of speech decoding, *Journal of Personality and Social Psychology* 6, 341–9.

Dittmann, A. T. and Llewellyn, L. G. (1968) Relationship between vocalization and head nods as listener responses, *Journal of Personality and Social Psychology* 11, 98–106.

Dittmann, A. T. and Wynne, L. C. (1961) Linguistic techniques and the analysis of emotionality in interviews, *Journal of Abnormal and Social Psychology* 63, 201–4.

Duncan, S. (1972) Some signals and rules for taking speaking turns in conversations, *Journal of Personality and Social Psychology* 23, 283–92.

Duncan, S. (1973) Toward a grammar for dyadic conversation, *Semiotica* 9, 29–47.

Duncan, S. (1974) On the structure of speaker–auditor interaction during speaking turns, *Language in Society* 2, 161–80.

Duncan, S. (1975) Interaction units during speaking turns in dyadic face-to-face conversations, in A. Kendon, R.M. Harris and M.R. Key (eds.), *The Organization of Behaviour in Face-to-Face Interaction*, The Hague: Mouton.

Duncan, S. and Fiske, D. W. (1977) *Face-to-Face Interaction: Research, Methods and Theory*, New Jersey: Lawrence Erlbaum.

Edgington, E. S. (1972) A normal curve method for combining probability values from independent experiments, *Journal of Psychology* 82, 85–9.

Ehrlichman, H. (1981) From gaze aversion to eye movement suppression: an investigation of the cognitive interference explanation of gaze patterns during conversation, *British Journal of Social and Clinical Psychology* 20, 233–41.

Ehrlichman, H., Weiner, S. L. and Baker, A. H. (1974) Effects of verbal and spatial questions on initial gaze shifts, *Neuropsychologia* 12, 265–77.

Ekman, P. and Friesen, W. V. (1969) The repertoire of nonverbal behaviour: categories, origins, usage and coding, *Semiotica* 1, 49–98.

Elzinga, R. H. (1978a) Temporal organization of conversation, *Sociolinguistics Newsletter* 9 (2), 29–31.

Elzinga, R. H. (1978b) Temporal aspects of Japanese and Australian conversation. Unpublished Ph.D. dissertation, Australian National University, Canberra.

Esposito, A. (1979) Sex differences in children's conversation, *Language and Speech* 22, 213–21.

Exline, R. V. (1971) Visual interaction: the glances of power and preference, *Nebraska Symposium on Motivation*, 163–206.

Exline, R. V. and Eldridge, C. (1967) Effects of two patterns of a speaker's visual behaviour upon the authenticity of his verbal message, Paper presented to the Eastern Psychological Association, Boston.

Exline, R. V. and Winters, L. C. (1965) Effects of cognitive difficulty and cognitive style upon eye contact in interviews, Paper read to the Eastern Psychological Association.

Farina, A. (1960) Patterns of role dominance and conflict in parents of schizophrenic patients, *Journal of Abnormal and Social Psychology* **61**, 31–8.

Feldman, S. S. (1959) *Mannerisms of Speech and Gesture in Everyday Life*, New York: International Universities Press.

Feldstein, S., Alberti, L., Ben Debba, M. and Welkowitz, J. (1974) Personality and simultaneous speech, Paper presented at the annual meeting of the American Psychological Association, New Orleans.

Feldstein, S. and Welkowitz, J. (1978) A chronography of conversation: in defense of an objective approach, in A. W. Siegman and S. Feldstein (eds.), *Nonverbal Behavior and Communication*, New Jersey: Lawrence Erlbaum.

Ferguson, N. (1976) Interruptions: speaker-switch nonfluency in spontaneous conversation, Edinburgh University, Department of Linguistics, *Work in Progress* **9**, 1–19.

Ferguson, N. (1977) Simultaneous speech, interruptions and dominance, *British Journal of Social and Clinical Psychology* **16**, 295–302.

Fodor, J. A., Bever, T. G. and Garrett, M. F. (1974) *The Psychology of Language*, New York: McGraw-Hill.

Forbes, R. J. and Jackson, P. R. (1980) Non-verbal behaviour and the outcome of selection interviews, *Journal of Occupational Psychology* **53**, 65–72.

Freedle, R. and Lewis, M. (1977) Prelinguistic conversations, in M. Lewis and R. Freedle (eds.), *Interaction, Conversation and the Development of Language*, New York: Wiley.

Freedman, N. and Hoffman, S. P. (1967) Kinetic behavior in altered clinical states: an approach to objective analysis of motor behavior during clinical interviews, *Perceptual and Motor Skills* **24**, 527–39.

Freud, S. (1905) Fragments of an analysis of a case of hysteria, reprinted in J. Strachey (ed.) *The Standard Edition of the Complete Psychological Works of Sigmund Freud. Vol 7*, (1953) London: Hogarth Press.

Gale, A., Lucas, B., Nissim, R. and Harpham, B. (1972) Some EEG correlates of face-to-face contact, *British Journal of Social and Clinical Psychology* **11**, 326–32.

Gallois, C. and Markel, N. N. (1975) Turn taking: social personality and conversational style, *Journal of Personality and Social Psychology* **31**, 1134–40.

Garfinkel, H. (1967) *Studies in Ethnomethodology* New Jersey: Prentice-Hall.

Ginett, L. E. and Moran, L. J. (1964) Stability of vocabulary performance by schizophrenics, *Journal of Consulting Psychology* **28**, 178–9.

Goffman, E. (1981) *Forms of Talk*, Oxford: Basil Blackwell.

Goldman-Eisler, F. (1958a) Speech production and the predictability of words in context, *Quarterly Journal of Experimental Psychology* 10, 96–106.

Goldman-Eisler, F. (1958b) The predictability of words in context and the length of pauses in speech, *Language and Speech* 1, 226–31.

Goldman-Eisler, F. (1967) Sequential temporal patterns and cognitive processes in speech, *Language and Speech* 10, 122–32.

Goldman-Eisler, F. (1968) *Psycholinguistics: Experiments in Spontaneous Speech*, London: Academic Press.

Goldman-Eisler, F. (1972) Pauses, clauses, sentences, *Language and Speech* 15, 103–13.

Graham, J. A. and Argyle, M. (1975) A cross-cultural study of the communication of extra-verbal meaning by gestures, *Journal of Human Movement Studies* 1, 33–9.

Graham, J. A. and Heywood, S. (1975) The effects of elimination of hand gestures and of verbal codability on speech performance, *European Journal of Social Psychology* 5, 189–95.

Hall, J. A. (1978) Gender effects in decoding nonverbal cues, *Psychological Bulletin* 85, 845–57.

Hall, J. A. (1979) Gender, gender roles and nonverbal communication skills, in R. Rosenthal (ed.), *Skill in nonverbal communication: individual differences*, Cambridge, Mass.: Oelgeschlager, Gunn and Hain.

Halliday, M. A. K. and Hasan, R. (1976) *Cohesion in English*, Hong Kong: Longman.

Hatano, G., Miyake, Y. and Binks, M. G. (1977) Performance of expert abacus operators, *Cognition* 5, 57–71.

Hawkins, P. R. (1973) The influence of sex, social class and pause-location in the hesitation phenomena of seven-year-old children, in B. Bernstein (ed.), *Class, Codes and Control*, vol. 2, London: Routledge & Kegan Paul.

Hedge, B. J., Everitt, B. S. and Frith, C. D. (1978) The role of gaze in dialogue, *Acta Psychologia* 42, 453–75.

Henderson, A., Goldman-Eisler, F. and Skarbek, A. (1966) Sequential temporal patterns in spontaneous speech, *Language and Speech* 9, 207–16.

Hetherington, E. M., Stouwie, R. J. and Ridberg, E. H. (1971) Patterns of family interaction and child-rearing attitudes related to three dimensions of juvenile delinquency, *Journal of Abnormal Psychology* 75, 160–76.

Jackson, H. J. (1878) On affectations of speech from disease of the brain. Reprinted in *Selected Writings of Hughlings Jackson* (1958), vol. 2, 155–70, New York: Basic Books.

Jacob, T. (1974) Patterns of family conflict and dominance as a function of child age and social class, *Developmental Psychology* 10, 1–12.

Jacob, T. (1975) Family interaction in disturbed and normal families: a methodological and substantive review, *Psychological Bulletin* 82, 33–65.

Jaffe, J., Breskin, S. and Gerstman, L. J. (1972) Random generation of apparent speech rhythms, *Language and Speech* 15, 68–71.

Jaffe, J. and Feldstein, S. (1970) *Rhythms of Dialogue*, New York: Academic Press.

Jefferson, G. (1973) A case of precision timing in ordinary conversation:

overlapped tag-positioned address terms in closing sequences, *Semiotica* **9**, 47–96.

Kasl, S. V. and Mahl, G. E. (1965) The relationship of disturbances and hesitations in spontaneous speech to anxiety, *Journal of Personality and Social Psychology* **1**, 425–33.

Kendon, A. (1967) Some functions of gaze direction in social interaction, *Acta Psychologica* **26**, 22–63.

Kendon, A. (1972) Some relationships between body motion and speech. An analysis of an example, in A. W. Siegman and B. Pope (eds.), *Studies in Dyadic Communication*, New York: Pergamon.

Kendon, A. (1978) Looking in conversation and the regulation of turns at talk: a comment on the papers of G. Beattie and D. R. Rutter *et al.*, *British Journal of Social and Clinical Psychology* **17**, 23–4.

Kendon, A. and Cook, M. (1969) The consistency of gaze patterns in social interaction, *British Journal of Psychology* **69**, 481–94.

Kleck, R. E. and Nuessle, W. (1968) Congruence between the indicative and communicative functions of eye-contact in interpersonal relations, *British Journal of Social and Clinical Psychology* **7**, 241–6.

Kleinke, C. L. and Pohlen, P. D. (1971) Affective and emotional responses as a function of other person's gaze and cooperativeness in a two-person game, *Journal of Personality and Social Psychology* **17**, 308–13.

Knight, D. J., Langmeter, D. L. and Landgren, D. C. (1973) Eye-contact, distance and affiliation: the role of observer bias, *Sociometry* **36**, 390–401.

Kozhevnikov, V. A. and Chistovich, L. A. (1965) Speech articulation and perception, US Dept. of Commerce, Joint Publication Research Service, Washington, DC.

Krauss, R. M., Apple, W., Morency, N., Wenzel, C. and Winton, W. (1981) Verbal, vocal and visible factors in judgement of another's affect, *Journal of Personality and Social Psychology* **40**, 312–20.

Lackner, J. R. and Tuller, B. (1976) The influence of syntactic segmentation on perceived stress, *Cognition* **4**, 303–7.

Lalljee, M. G. and Cook, M. (1969) An experimental investigation of the function of filled pauses in speech, *Language and speech* **12**, 24–28.

La Russo, L. (1978) Sensitivity of Paranoid Patients to Nonverbal Cues, *Journal of Abnormal Psychology* **87**, 463–471.

Lay, C. H. and Burron, B. F. (1968) Perception of the personality of the hesitant speaker, *Perception and Motor Skills* **26**, 951–6.

Leach, C. (1979) *Introduction to Statistics: A Nonparametric Approach for the Social Sciences*, Chichester: Wiley.

Leathers, D. G. (1976) *Nonverbal Communication Systems*, Boston: Allyn and Bacon.

Lefcourt, H. M., Rotenberg, F., Buckspan, P. and Steffy, R. A. (1967) Visual interaction and performance of process and reactive schizophrenics as a function of examiner's sex, *Journal of Personality* **35**, 535–46.

Libby, W. L. (1970) Eye contact and direction of looking as stable individual differences, *Journal of Experimental Research in Personality* **4**, 303–12.

Libet, J. M. and Lewinsohn, P. M. (1973) Concept of social skill with special reference to the behavior of depressed persons, *Journal of Consulting and Clinical Psychology* **40**, 304–12.

Lieberman, P. (1965) On the acoustic basis of the perception of intonation by linguists, *Word* **21**, 40–54.

Long, J. M. (1972) Biosocial factors in conversational interaction. Unpublished master's thesis, University of Florida.

Lounsbury, F. G. (1954) Transitional probability, linguistic structure and systems of habit-family hierarchies, in C. E. Osgood and T. A. Sebeok (eds.), *Psycholinguistics: A Survey of Theory and Research Problems*, Indiana: University Press.

Lyons, J. (1972) Human Language, in R. A. Hinde (ed.), *Non-Verbal Communication*, Cambridge: CUP.

McDowall, J. J. (1978) Interactional synchrony: a reappraisal, *Journal of Personality and Social Psychology* **36**, 963–75.

Maclay, H. and Osgood, C. E. (1959) Hesitation phenomena in spontaneous English speech, *Word* **15**, 19–44.

McNeill, D. (1975) Semiotic extension, in R. L. Solso (ed.), *Information Processing and Cognition: The Loyola Symposium*, Hillsdale, New Jersey: Lawrence Erlbaum.

McNeill, D. (1979) *The Conceptual Basis of Language*, New Jersey: Lawrence Erlbaum.

Mahl, G. F., Danet, B. and Norton, N. (1959) Reflection of major personality characteristics in gestures and body movement, Paper presented at the Annual Meeting of the American Psychological Association, Cincinnati, Ohio.

Martin, J. G. (1970) On judging pauses in spontaneous speech, *Journal of Verbal Learning and Verbal Behaviour* **9**, 75–8.

Marzillier, J. S. and Winter, K. (1978) Success and failure in social skills training: individual differences, *Behaviour Research and Therapy* **16**, 67–84.

Matarazzo, J. D. and Saslow, G. (1961) Differences in interview interaction behaviour among normal and deviant groups, in I. A. Berg and R. M. Bass (eds.), *Conformity and Deviation*, New York: Harper Row.

Mayo, C. and La France, M. (1978) On the acquisition of nonverbal communication: a review, *Merrill–Palmer Quarterly* **24**, 213–28.

Mehrabian, A. (1972) *Nonverbal Communication*, Chicago: Aldine.

Mehrabian, A. and Ferris, S. R. (1967) Inference of attitudes from nonverbal communication in two channels, *Journal of Consulting Psychology* **31**, 248–52.

Mehrabian, A. and Wiener, M. (1967) Decoding of inconsistent communications, *Journal of Personality and Social Psychology* **6**, 109–14.

Meltzer, L., Morris, W. N. and Hayes, D. P. (1971) Interruption outcomes and vocal amplitude: Explorations in social psychophysics, *Journal of Personality and Social Psychology* **18**, 392–402.

Mercer, N. McK. (1976) Frequency and availability in the encoding of spontaneous speech, *Language and Speech* **19**, 129–43.

Miller, G. A. (1963) Review of Greenberg, J. H. (ed.) *Universals of Language, Contemporary Psychology* **8**, 417–18.

Mishler, E. G. and Waxler, N. E. (1968) *Interaction in Families: An Experimental Study of Family Processes and Schizophrenia*, New York: Wiley.

Moran, L. T., Gorham, D. R. and Holtzman, W. H. (1960) Vocabulary knowledge and usage of schizophrenic subjects: a six-year follow-up, *Journal of Abnormal and Social Psychology* **61**, 246–54.

Natale, M. (1976) A Markovian model of adult gaze behaviour, *Journal of Psycholinguistics Research* **5**, 53–63.

Natale, M., Entin, E. and Jaffe, J. (1979) Vocal interruptions in dyadic communication as a function of speech and social anxiety, *Journal of Personality and Social Psychology* **37**, 865–78.

Nichols, K. A. and Champness, B. G. (1971) Eye gaze and the GSR, *Journal of Experimental Social Psychology* **7**, 623–6.

Nielsen, G. (1962) *Studies in Self Confrontation*, Copenhagen: Monksgaard.

Oldfield, R. C. and Wingfield, A. (1965) Response latencies in naming objects, *Quarterly Journal of Experimental Psychology* **4**, 273–81.

Patterson, M. L. (1973) Stability of non-verbal immediacy behaviours, *Journal of Experimental Social Psychology* **9**, 97–109.

Patterson, M. L. (1976) An arousal model of interpersonal intimacy, *Psychological Review* **83**, 235–45.

Pilkonis, P. A. (1977) The behavioural consequences of shyness, *Journal of Personality* **45**, 596–611.

Reich, S. S. (1975) The function of pauses for the decoding of speech. Unpublished Ph.D. thesis, University College London.

Reynolds, A. and Paivio, A. (1968) Cognitive and emotional determinants of speech, *Canadian Journal of Psychology* **22**, 164–75.

Riemer, M. D. (1949) The averted gaze, *Psychiatric Quarterly* **23**, 108–15.

Riemer, M. D. (1955) Abnormalities of gaze – a classification, *Psychiatric Quarterly* **29**, 659–72.

Rim, Y. (1977) Personality variables and interruptions in small group discussions, *European Journal of Social Psychology* **7**, 247–51.

Rimé, B. and McCusker, L. (1976) Visual behaviour in social interaction: the validity of eye-contact assessments under different conditions of observation, *British Journal of Psychology* **67**, 507–14.

Robbins, O., Devoe, S. and Wiener, M. (1978) Social patterns of turn-taking: nonverbal regulators, *Journal of Communication* **28**, 38–46.

Rochester, S. R. (1973) The significance of pauses in spontaneous speech, *Journal of Psycholinguistic Research* **2**, 51–81.

Rosenfeld, H. M. (1978) Conversational control functions of nonverbal behavior, in A. W. Siegman and S. Feldstein (eds.), *Nonverbal Behavior and Communication*, Hillsdale, New Jersey: Lawrence Erlbaum.

Rosenthal, R. (1978) Combining results of independent studies, *Psychological Bulletin* **85**, 185–93.

Rosenthal, R. (1979) Conducting judgement studies, Paper presented to the

Advanced Study Institute on 'Methods of Research in Nonverbal Communication', Birkbeck College, London.

Ross, L. (1977) Shortcomings of the intuitive psychologist, *Advances in Experimental Social Psychology* **10**, 174–214.

Ross, L., Green, D. and House, P. (1977) The 'False Consensus Effect': An egocentric bias in social perception and attributional processes, *Journal of Experimental Social Psychology* **13**, 279–301.

Rutter, D. R. (1973) Visual interaction in psychiatric patients: a review, *British Journal of Psychiatry* **23**, 193–202.

Rutter, D. R. (1976) Visual interaction in recently admitted and chronic long-stay schizophrenic patients, *British Journal of Social and Clinical Psychology* **15**, 295–305.

Rutter, D. R. (1977a) Speech patterning in recently admitted and chronic long-stay schizophrenic patients, *British Journal of Social and Clinical Psychology* **16**, 47–55.

Rutter, D. R. (1977b) Visual interaction and speech patterning in remitted and acute schizophrenic patients, *British Journal of Social and Clinical Psychology* **16**, 357–61.

Rutter, D. R. (1978) Visual interaction in schizophrenic patients: the timing of looks, *British Journal of Social and Clinical Psychology* **17**, 281–2.

Rutter, D. R. and Stephenson, G. M. (1972) Visual interaction in a group of schizophrenic and depressive patients, *British Journal of Social and Clinical Psychology* **11**, 57–65.

Rutter, D. R. and Stephenson, G. M. (1977) The role of visual communication in synchronising conversation, *European Journal of Social Psychology* **7**, 29–37.

Rutter, D. R., Stephenson, G. M., Ayling, K. and White, P. A. (1978) The timing of looks in dyadic conversation, *British Journal of Social and Clinical Psychology* **17**, 17–21.

Sacks, H., Schegloff, E. A. and Jefferson, G. A. (1974) A simplest systematics for the organization of turn-taking in conversation, *Language* **50**, 697–735.

Scheflen, A. E. (1964) The significance of posture in communication systems, *Psychiatry* **27**, 316–331.

Scheflen, A. E. (1965) Quasi courtship behavior in psychotherapy, *Psychiatry* **28**, 245–57.

Schegloff, E. A. and Sacks, H. (1973) Opening up closings, *Semiotica* **8**, 289–327.

Schlauch, M. (1936) Recent Soviet studies in linguistics *Sc. Soc.* **1**, 157.

Schulze, R. and Barefoot, J. (1974) Non-verbal responses and affiliative conflict theory, *British Journal of Social and Clinical Psychology* **13**, 237–43.

Short, J., Williams, E. and Christie, B. (1976) *The Social Psychology of Telecommunications*, London: Wiley.

Snow, C. E. and Ferguson, C. A. (1977) *Talking to Children*, Cambridge: Cambridge University Press.

Sokal, R. R. and Rohlf, F. J. (1973) *Introduction to Biostatistics*, San Francisco: W. H. Freeman.

Spelke, E., Hirst, W. and Neisser, U. (1976) Skills of divided attention, *Cognition* 4, 215–30.

Stephenson, G. M. and Rutter, D. R. (1970) Eye-contact, distance and affiliation: a re-evaluation, *British Journal of Psychology* 61, 385–93.

Stephenson, G. M., Rutter, D. R. and Dore, S. R. (1973) Visual interaction and distance, *British Journal of Psychology* 64, 251–7.

Stern, D. N. (1974) Mother and infant at play: the dyadic interaction involving facial, vocal and gaze behaviour, in M. Lewis and L. A. Rosenblum (eds.), *The Effect of the Infant on its Caregiver*, New York: Wiley.

Stern, D. N., Jaffe, J., Beebe, B. and Bennett, S. L. (1975) Vocalizing in unison and in alternation: two modes of communication within the mother–infant dyad, *Annals of the New York Academy of Sciences* 263, 89–100.

Tarone, E. (1975) Aspects of intonation in Black English, *American Speech* 48, 29–36.

Taylor, I. (1969) Content and structure in sentence production, *Journal of Verbal Learning and Verbal Behaviour* 8, 170–5.

Taylor, W. L. (1953) 'Cloze' procedure: a new tool for measuring readability, *Journalism Quarterly* 30, 415–33.

Trager, G. L. and Smith, H. L. (1951) An outline of English structure, *Studies in Linguistics*, occasional paper no. 3, Oklahoma: Norman.

Trevarthen, C. (1977) Descriptive analyses of infant communicative behaviour, in H. R. Schaffer (ed.), *Studies in Mother–Infant Interaction*, London: Academic Press.

Trower, P. (1980) Situational analysis of the components and processes of behavior of socially skilled and unskilled patients, *Journal of Consulting and Clinical Psychology* 48, 327–39.

Trower, P., Bryant, B. and Argyle, M. (1978) *Social Skills and Mental Health*, London: Methuen.

Turner, J. le B. (1964) Schizophrenics as judges of vocal expressions of emotional meanings, in J. R. Davitz (ed.), *The Communication of Emotional Meanings*, New York: McGraw-Hill.

Valian, V. V. (1971) Talking, listening and linguistic structure. Unpublished Ph.D. thesis, Northeastern University.

Van Dijk, T. A. (1977) *Text and Context: Explorations in the Semantics and Pragmatics of Discourse*, London: Longman.

Vuchinich, S. (1977) Elements of cohesion between turns in ordinary conversation, *Semiotica* 30, 229–57.

Weiner, S. L. and Ehrlichman, H. (1976) Ocular motility and cognitive process, *Cognition* 4, 31–43.

Weisbrod, R. R. (1965) Looking behavior in a discussion group. Cited by Kendon (1967).

Welkowitz, J., Cariffe, G. and Feldstein, S. (1976) Conversational congruence as a criterion of socialization in children, *Child Development* 47, 269–72.

Wiemann, J. M. and Knapp, M. L. (1975) Turn-taking in conversation, *Journal of Communication* 25, 75–92.

Winer, B. J. (1962) *Statistical Principles in Experimental Design*, New York: McGraw-Hill.

Yngve, V. H. (1970) On getting a word in edgewise, *Papers from the sixth regional meeting of the Chicago Linguistic Society*, Chicago: Chicago Linguistic Society.

Zimmerman, D. H. and West, C. (1975) Sex roles, interruptions and silences in conversation, in B. Thorne and N. Henley (eds.), *Language and Sex. Difference and Dominance*, Rowley, Mass.: Newbury House.

Subject Index

Name Index